The Unfolding Story of God's Salvation Plan

12 Life-Changing Personal or Group Studies

The Unfolding Story of God's Salvation Plan

12 Life-Changing Personal or Group Studies

MELVIN E. BANKS, LITT.D., EDITOR

Based on Selected Old Testament Scriptures

Urban Ministries, Inc.

Copyright © 2020 by Melvin E. Banks, LITT.D., Editor
All rights reserved.

First printing 1989; second printing 1993; third printing 1994; fourth printing 1998.

No part of this book may be reproduced or transmitted in any form or by any means, electronic or mechanical, including photocopying, recording, video, or by any information or retrieval system, without prior written permission from the publisher except for the use of brief quotations in a book review.

Our thanks to the following persons whose writing contributions enabled us to prepare this volume of life-transforming Bible studies: Drs. Colleen Birchett (Ph.D.), Bennie Goodwin (Ph.D.), Kenneth Hammond (Ed.D.), Philip Rodman (M.A.), and Cynthia Forn.

Published in the United States by Urban Ministries, Inc.
P. O. Box 436987
Chicago, IL 60643
www.urbanministries.com 1-800-860-8642

ISBN 978-1-68353-670-3 (paperback)
ISBN 978-1-68353-669-7 (eBook)

Unless otherwise noted, Scripture texts are taken from the King James Version of the Bible. Other versions quoted include the following:

LB—Living Bible, c. 1971
NIV—New International Version, c. 1973, 1978, 1984
RSV—The Revised Standard Version, c. 1952, 1971

Cover design by Laura Duffy Design
Book design by Amit Dey

Printed in the United States of America.

TABLE OF CONTENTS

Preface vii
Foreword xiii
Introduction. xv
Bible Study Guides
   1. The Prologue. 1
   2. The Origin of Sin 10
   3. God Sets His People Free. 19
   4. God Covenants with His People 30
   5. What Do These Stones Mean?. 42
   6. A Tragic Cycle. 53
   7. Seizing An Opportunity 65
   8. A House Divided. 74
   9. God Uses Obedient People 82
  10. A Call for Justice and Righteousness 90
  11. God Promises to Bless. 102
  12. God Gives New Life 113
About the Author. 125

Preface

How To Use This Book

The materials in these studies provide for in-depth exploration of the Scriptures. At the same time, we recognize that merely studying Bible texts as an end in itself is not adequate to accomplish all that should be accomplished.

The Scriptures make clear that God's purpose for people is that first they would come to know Him as Saviour (2 Peter 3:9), then go on to develop their relationship with Him so their lifestyles increasingly reflect the likeness of Jesus Christ (1 Peter 2:2).

We read in Romans 8:29 that God "predestinated [us] to be conformed to the image of His Son..." In other words, God's desire for believers is that they become more and more like Jesus Christ in character. Of course, we know that Jesus Christ is perfect and that we will never reach ultimate perfection in this lifetime. At the same time, the Bible encourages us to pursue the likeness of Christ. Note the purpose of each of the following sections which appear throughout the studies:

- DEFINING THE ISSUE
- AIM
- SCRIPTURE TEXT

- BIBLE BACKGROUND
- POINTS TO PONDER
- LESSON AT-A-GLANCE
- EXPLORING THE MEANING
- DISCERNING MY DUTY
- DECIDING MY RESPONSE
- LIGHT ON THE HEAVY

DEFINING THE ISSUE

These studies are designed to help people grow in their relationship with Jesus Christ—to foster discipleship. Each study begins with a section we call "DEFINING THE ISSUE." The purpose of this is to elevate a life need which will be addressed in the exploration of the Scripture text.

Scholars have observed that every book in the Bible was written to address a life need of the people to whom the book is addressed—whether to document their history, deal with a false doctrine, or encourage holiness of life.

AIM

This is a statement of what the study is designed to accomplish in the life of the participant. Aims can be modified to address the specific needs which the leader of the group senses to be those of the participants. A leader should never feel that the suggested aim has to be slavishly adhered to. The study is a "guide," not an unchangeable formula.

The aims are structured to address the cognitive, emotional, and volitional components of behavioral change. Participants are encouraged to KNOW the truth, to FEEL deeply about the truth, and to take ACTION which reinforces the truth. All of this leads to a change in behavior—spiritual growth.

SCRIPTURE TEXT

This section includes a printed portion of Scripture upon which the study focuses. While the studies were prepared using the King James Version of the Bible, any version that the group prefers can be used.

BIBLE BACKGROUND

This section provides contextual material which can aid in understanding the people to whom the Scripture was originally addressed. It also explains the context for the Scripture portion, so the text is easier to grasp.

POINTS TO PONDER

These questions are designed to help focus the minds of participants on some of the areas the study will address and to facilitate understanding the text.

LESSON AT A GLANCE

This section is an outline of the text which facilitates dividing the Scripture into smaller segments.

EXPLORING THE MEANING

Comments on the Scripture texts will be found in this section. If possible, participants will have read this material prior to the gathering so that reading entire sections is not necessary. However, the leader may want portions to be read in order to reinforce a particular point of discussion.

DISCERNING MY DUTY

Since the discussion of meaning should not be an end in itself, we have provided a section entitled, "DISCERNING MY DUTY." While in many cases this allows the participant to think about individual responses to the Scripture, occasionally this exercise may focus on group action. This is especially helpful if you think of your group as more than a "study" group. That is, your people will occasionally want to collectively engage in some activity which reinforces the aim of the study and, at the same time, promote the welfare of others.

DECIDING MY RESPONSE

Since there is a difference between knowing what could be done and actually doing it, "DECIDING MY RESPONSE" allows a participant to pinpoint what his response will be as a result of discovering what could be done.

We believe this approach to the study of Scripture will not only be exciting to all the participants but will result in real spiritual growth—discipleship.

LIGHT ON THE HEAVY

This section will provide additional information on a word or theme deemed helpful to the readers.

OTHER SUGGESTIONS

1. *As a way of strengthening the bonds among people within your group, you may want to plan some kind of social event once per quarter. This may consist of a potluck supper, a dinner, or some type of group outing, for example.*

2. *You may want to consider some form of ministry activity during the course of a study, such as one of the following:*
    - *Conduct a jail or prison service.*
    - *Make or purchase gifts for a public or private school class.*
    - *Organize a special church cleaning.*
    - *Conduct a fundraising project for a missionary.*
    - *Gather clothing for needy children.*
    - *Write letters to a politician on a local or national issue of morality or justice.*
    - *Raise funds to send a needy child to a summer camp or on vacation.*

    A little time spent brainstorming in your group will produce lots of other ideas for serving the Lord and people in a practical way.

3. *You may want to use a portion of your time to allow your group members to pray for one another and for needs of the church.*

Foreword

CELEBRATE 50 YEARS WITH US!

When UMI began in 1970, African Americans were still struggling to undo the effects of 350 years of slavery and Jim Crow segregation.

We believed both then and now that the more we know and rely on God's revelation in the Bible, the more we will be equipped to serve Him and to deal with racism, injustice, and to represent Jesus Christ in our world.

Three books, *The Unfolding Story of God's Salvation Plan*, *God Delivers on His Promise*, and *Good News about Jesus Christ*, are examples of UMI Bible studies that enrich our knowledge of God's Word. In these and other Bible studies, we explore not only our need for personal holiness but also God's standards for social justice and righteous living.

Since 1970, life has improved for many African Americans. Yes, we have a long way to go, but we see progress. Many churches have enriched their Christian educational programs. Surveys show that today a high number of young adults cling to the church and the Christian faith to help them cope with injustice and to live right. UMI's approach in presenting biblical truth improves total growth by offering Bible studies contextualized and professionally produced for African American children, youth, and adults.

It gives me great joy to see how God is using these materials to transform people for His eternal purposes.

It is clear that the mode of teaching is changing from analog to digital. This rapid change challenges churches to upgrade communication methods to accommodate digitized content. We know God's truth will never change because God is eternal truth. Still, our ways of teaching must adjust to a changing culture. For the 50th anniversary edition, these three books, which were originally published in print only, are now available as eBooks. We hope to see millions of more people come to love and live for our Lord in the years ahead.

African Americans are conscious of our African roots, and we seek to connect with brothers and sisters on the continent and in the African diaspora. Together we can have a greater impact on the world for Christ and His eternal kingdom.

Carl Jeffrey Wright
Chief Executive Officer
Urban Ministries, Inc.
Chicago, Illinois
September 8, 2020

Introduction

The Unfolding of God's Redemptive Plan

The unfolding of God's plan to bring salvation to the world is a most fascinating drama. We read in Genesis that God created humankind in His own image and likeness. That in itself boggles the mind. Think about it. Here is God, infinitely intelligent, perfectly holy, totally self-sufficient, yet choosing to create human beings with the capacity of thinking His thoughts behind Him, capable of having fellowship with the Creator, and with a free will to choose whether or not to follow His will. What is so marvelous about this truth is that when we think of our spending eternity with God, it makes sense only if we have the capacity to share His glory and nature. He gave us that capacity when we were created.

In LESSON ONE, we focus on God's creative activity of bringing into existence the world and its content. The crowning act of creation was that of creating human beings in His own image.

But after being created in His image and likeness, we blew it. We sinned. LESSON TWO in this series focuses on the fall of humankind into sin.

God did not forget us when we sinned. The human race deteriorated to the point that God found it necessary to destroy humanity with a flood, but he saved the race by preserving Noah and his family to repopulate the earth. At the appropriate time, he selected Abraham and promised that through him He would bring redemption to all people of the earth (Genesis 22:15-18). Abraham's descendants developed into a nation some 400 years after the patriarch lived. Their enslavement by the Egyptians became God's opportunity to bring them out and establish a covenant with them. God chose Moses to lead the people out of bondage. He revealed Himself to Moses at the burning bush, and after a series of devastating plagues, God inflicted a blow that motivated the Pharaoh to let the people go. LESSON THREE focuses on this dramatic deliverance.

Delivering two million people is one thing, but molding them into a nation and giving them directions for living and worship is another. LESSON FOUR focuses on Sinaitic Covenant at which place God offered to be their God, and they vowed to be faithful in worship and obedience.

Despite all God's love and power in delivering the people from bondage, they chose to reject His offer to take them into the Promised Land. For this disobedience God decreed that none of that generation would enter the land. He waited until that generation had died out, and, under the leadership of Joshua, empowered their descendants to cross the Jordan. LESSON FIVE describes how God empowered their new leader Joshua to lead the people across the Jordan River. God instructed that a memorial be established to celebrate the crossing.

The people entered and conquered the land, but they were unable to displace the Hamitic people living there. Instead they intermarried with them and adopted their customs and worship. To discipline His people and call them back to faithfulness to the covenant, God allowed surrounding nations to afflict the people. When they cried out because of the severity of their affliction,

God raised up judges to deliver them. The recurring cycle of sin, judgment, groaning, and deliverance took the nation further and further from the covenant promises. This cycle is the theme of LESSON SIX.

In their state of rebellion, the people ask for a king. God permits them to have a king and gives Saul, son of Kish, the opportunity to become their first monarch. God tells Samuel, the judge and prophet at that time, "It is not you they have rejected, but they have rejected me as their king" (1 Samuel 8:7, NIV). Saul is anointed to be king. This is the focus of LESSON SEVEN.

But because he was unwilling to obey God and destroy the Amalekites whom God directed him to wipe out, God rejected Saul as king. Saul's dynasty ended, and God selected David, a man after His own heart. David was faithful to the Lord, even though at the height of his rule he fell into sin, committing adultery with Bathsheba and having her black Hittite husband murdered (see Genesis 10:15 where Heth is a reference to Hittites).

David's son, Solomon, was David's successor. During his rule the kingdom of Israel was at its zenith, its borders reaching from Egypt to the Euphrates River. Despite Solomon's wisdom and glory, he did not have sense enough to remain faithful to God. He turned to idolatry and God punished him by creating a split in the kingdom (1 Kings 11:29-33). After Solomon's death, his son Rehoboam precipitated this division by ignoring the advice of older men and accepting the advice of his peers. He vowed to inflict a greater burden of taxes and labor on the people than Solomon had done. This attitude resulted in a divided kingdom which has never been healed. This is the theme of LESSON EIGHT.

LESSON NINE illustrates how God uses obedient people to accomplish His purposes and bring help to people in need. The people moved further and further away from God's expectation of them. The rich began to exploit the poor, murder innocent people, commit adultery, and engage in all sorts of lewd behavior and idolatrous worship. God sent prophet after prophet to warn them of their grievous sins. Amos was one of these prophets. The heart of his message is the theme of LESSON TEN.

Frequent departure from the commands of God can largely be blamed on the failure of the leadership. These leaders had failed to faithfully proclaim God's message and accept their responsibilities for teaching and modeling of what God expected from His people. God used the prophet Ezekiel to remind the shepherds of their failures, promising that one day He would raise up a true Shepherd who would care for the sheep as God desired. This is the focus of LESSON ELEVEN.

God's judgment on the nation for its waywardness was exile. First the northern kingdom was sent into captivity in 722 B.C. The southern kingdom, too, eventually deteriorated to the point that God allowed the Babylonians to invade the land and deport thousands away. The people groaned and moaned under the heavy load of servitude to the Babylonians. Graciously, God permitted Ezekiel to prophesy of a day when God would restore the people. He would cause the dry bones to be resurrected. This promise of restoration is the theme of LESSON TWELVE.

The Prologue
Based on Genesis 1:1-2:3

DEFINING THE ISSUE

Because it is found at the very beginning of the Bible, the story of Creation is one of the most familiar parts of Scripture. It has been told, discussed, and debated in the earliest grades of Sunday School and in the most advanced classes of seminary. It is simple and yet profound. Its beauty is the subject of our lesson this week.

AIM

By the end of the study, students will have explored God's wisdom and power in bringing human beings into existence, will praise God for His relevant attributes, and will commit themselves to living for the glory of our Creator and Sustainer.

SCRIPTURE TEXT

> GENESIS 1:1 In the beginning God created the heaven and the earth.
>
> 1:26 And God said, Let us make man in our image, after our likeness: and let them have dominion over the fish of the sea, and over the fowl of the air, and over the

cattle, and over all the earth, and over every creeping thing that creepeth upon the earth.

27 So God created man in his own image, in the image of God created he him; male and female created he them.

28 And God blessed them, and God said unto them, Be fruitful, and multiply, and replenish the earth, and subdue it: and have dominion over the fish of the sea, and over the fowl of the air, and over every living thing that moveth upon the earth

29 And God said, Behold, I have given you every herb bearing seed, which is upon the face of all the earth, and every tree, in the which is the fruit of a tree yielding seed; to you it shall be for meat.

30 And to every beast of the earth, and to every fowl of the air, and to every thing that creepeth upon the earth, wherein there is life, I have given every green herb for meat: and it was so.

31 And God saw every thing that he had made, and, behold, it was very good. And the evening and the morning were the sixth day.

2:1 Thus the heavens and the earth were finished, and all the host of them.

2 And on the seventh day God ended his work which he had made; and he rested on the seventh day from all his work which he had made.

3 And God blessed the seventh day, and sanctified it: because that in it he had rested from all his work which God created and made.

BACKGROUND

Genesis is the book of "beginnings." It records the origins of all things in the physical realm, including the heavens and the earth, mankind, the Sabbath, work, marriage, sin, redemption, civil government, national entities, etc. The first chapter describes the beginning of the universe, the earth, the content of the earth, including human beings.

Many questions have been raised about Genesis 1. Can the biblical account be reconciled with science, especially the evolutionary theory? Were the days 24-hour days? Why do we read that light appeared on Day 1, before the sun, which appeared on Day 4? While some Bible scholars have found ways to reconcile certain aspects of science with the biblical account, most agree that the purpose of Genesis is not to be a scientific journal, but to inform us of WHO brought into existence all that is. That point is emphatically made several times: "God said . . ." and God acted.

Accurate science will never contradict a correct understanding of God's truth because God is the source of ALL truth. The conflict arises because scientists do not know everything. When scientific knowledge is more complete we will discover that remarkable harmony exists. Until then, we accept the truth of God's Word and wait in anticipation until science catches up!

This first lesson focuses on the beginning of mankind, created in the image of God. It sets the context for properly understanding God's dealings with people throughout the rest of the Bible.

POINTS TO PONDER

1. *What are the first four words of the Bible? (Genesis 1:1)*
2. *Over what things does mankind have dominion? (1:26)*

3. *God creates mankind to reflect what about Himself? (1:26, 27)*
4. *What was God's estimation about His creation? (1:31)*
5. *What did God do on and what did he do for the seventh day? (2:2-3)*

LESSON AT-A-GLANCE

1. *God's presence (Genesis 1:1)*
2. *God's priority (1:26-30)*
3. *God's perfection (1:31)*
4. *God's peace (2:1-3)*

EXPLORING THE MEANING

1. God's presence (Genesis 1:1)

The first four words of the Bible are presented in a very simple manner, and yet they have been the basis for endless volumes of theological writings. "In the beginning God…"! What a profound declaration! This first statement requires an expression of faith. Without such faith, the rest of the Scriptures have no meaning.

Genesis 1:1 makes no effort to prove that God exists. The story of Creation begins with the declaration that God *was* at the outset. Whenever things got started, God was there. Our minds may struggle with the idea of an eternal being. We cannot explain the concept. We accept the fact by faith. "He that cometh to God must believe that he is," and it is through faith that "we understand that the worlds were framed by the word of God" (Hebrews 11:6, 3).

The account of Creation should remind us that God is very close to this universe. The description given in Genesis 1 does not leave us with the sense that God holds the universe "at arm's length." Instead, He shows tenderness, involvement, concern, and a personal touch. That is why David says, "The earth is the Lord's" (Psalm 24:1). That is why we can sing, "This is my Father's world." It is God's "pride and joy." It is His personal work of science and art!

2. God's priority (1:26-30)

The supreme point in God's creation was the act of producing humanity. The message of the whole Bible is set forth in this very first chapter of Genesis. That message is that God loves humankind. We are a very special part of God's universe. There are many evidences of this truth in Genesis 1.

Notice how God creates mankind—male and female, "in our image, after our likeness" (v. 26). Mankind, by virtue of his form and nature, is something special. Just what this means is not altogether clear. We know that God is not confined to a physical form such as ours. However, it would seem that the Scriptures are telling us that we have certain mental, emotional, volitional, and certainly spiritual capabilities, many of which are different from those of animals.

Further, God makes it clear that man is to "have dominion" over the rest of those things which inhabit the earth (Genesis 1:26, 28). Since this dominion was given to both male and female together, and they were the only persons existing at the time, slavery and other forms of human oppression do not come within this purview.

God has blessed humans with the skills and intelligence to be good stewards over His creation. Dominion over the earth is closely related to mankind's means of survival, including the food we are to eat—fish, beasts of the earth, fowl, living things, every green herb (vv. 28, 30).

Our responsibilities as stewards demand that we value each other. We are called to care for each other as well as our earth. People are the crown of God's creation—we must treat them as such. If you take better care of your cat than you do of your neighbor, your priorities are skewed! If you are more concerned about your church building than about your church members (or those outside the church!), your values are distorted. Evaluate where you spend your time and money. Does it reflect what you say you believe is important?

3. God's perfection (1:31)

Seven times during the process of creating the heavens and the earth, God paused to examine His work. Each time, the Bible tells us that He "saw that it was good." In fact, when He was finished, He said that it was "very good" (v. 31). This is a strong affirmation of God's work. He does all things well!

Some people question the world God has made. They ask, "Why did God allow man to sin?" "Why did God permit suffering and death to enter the experience of man?" Of course, God could have created a being that did not have the capacity to sin. God could have made a being that did not have the ability to choose between good and evil. Instead, in His wisdom, He chose to make humans just as they are. And God said that His creation was "good."

God could call creation "good" because He knew its nature, He made it and placed into it every sort of excellence suitable for it. Also, God could see the end from the beginning. He knew that the same power which brought about the universe would redeem and restore it when it became marred by sin. God knew from the beginning that Jesus Christ, who shared in the work of creation (John 1:10; Colossians 1:16), would also share in the work of redemption (Hebrews 2:9).

4. God's peace (2:1-3)

The fact that God "rested from all His work" does not mean that God needed rest for Himself. Rather, it was symbolic of what God wants and has for us. Perhaps the most important lesson here is that God wants us to follow His example and take time out to contemplate the things that He has done. He wants us to "be still, and know that I am God" (Psalm 46:10). Lives too busy are often empty lives. They also are void of true worship. Take a break! Reflect on God's glory in the people and creation surrounding your life.

The fact that God rested has an even larger meaning. It speaks to us of the finished work of Christ. Hebrews 1:3 tells us, "[W]hen [Christ] had by himself purged our sins, [he] sat down on the right hand of the Majesty on high...." There were no seats in the Old Testament temples because the priests' work was never complete. "But this man, after he had offered one sacrifice for sins for ever [His own life], sat down on the right hand of God" (Hebrews 10:12). His work was complete.

Finally, the fact that God rested from the work of creation speaks to us of a day when we shall have perfect rest with Him. At present, we have temporary vacations. In that day, "every day will be Sunday and the Sabbath will have no end." The writer of Hebrews tells us that, "we who believe God can enter into his place of rest" (Hebrews 4:3, LB). Faced with the tremendous difficulties we experience on this earth, it would be a shame to miss out on our eternal rest in heaven.

"God saw everything that he had made, and behold, it was very good" (Genesis 1:31, RSV).

DISCERNING MY DUTY

1. *What makes mankind different from animals?*
2. *Who was God talking with when he said, "Let us…"? (1:26)*
3. *Did God give females the same place as males in creation? (1:28)*
4. *What is the significance of God's blessing upon mankind?*
5. *When God said everything He made was "good," did He include Black people? Explain.*
6. *In what ways can people honor the Sabbath as God did?*

DECIDING MY RESPONSE

It is self-evident to Christians who believe the Bible that all people originated from God. It is important that each Christian understand the significance of this truth. For example, all people are indeed related one to another. All people have value, since all bear the image and likeness of God. All people are beautiful before God, though all people are not beautiful one to the other.

During the week, set aside a period of time to thank and praise the Lord for the way he made you—your race, color, physique, height, weight, feet length, eye-color, ears shape, complexion, everything!

WHAT I WILL DO

_____
_____
_____
_____
_____
_____

LIGHT ON THE HEAVY

HIS OWN IMAGE—Various suggestions have been made as to what is meant by the statement that human beings are made in the image and likeness of God. God is spirit so the reference includes intellectual, emotional, volitional, moral, self-determining, and social qualities.

The Origin of Sin
Based on Genesis 3:1-13

DEFINING THE ISSUE

Leslie's son is two years old and already mischievous. She is constantly running after him, moving things out of his way. Recently, Leslie had to spank her child's hand because he refused to obey her when she told him not to pick up a vase on the coffee table.

Leslie confided in her mother about her child's behavior. But her mother quickly assured her that the boy was only acting natural. Many children his age must be taught what it means when mother says no. Leslie's mother helped her see that the toddler had an innate nature toward stubbornness and disobedience, and Leslie would have to work with her child in overcoming this problem at an early age.

Human beings are born with a propensity to be rebellious, disobedient and sinful. Where did this nature come from? Why were we born sinners? (See Psalm 51:5.) Perhaps we cannot fully answer these questions. But one thing is sure: unless we are reborn with a new spiritual nature, our old human nature will continue to rebel.

In this Bible Study, we will focus on the origin of sin. As a result of Adam and Eve's sin, all human beings are infected with the "virus" of sin and follow their bad example.

AIM

By the end of the lesson students will be able to explain the origin of human sin and some of its personal and social consequences; will explore some solutions to social problems such as racism, poverty, and war that are the result of personal and corporate sin; and will examine their own lives, confess their sins, and accept God's forgiveness.

SCRIPTURE TEXT

GENESIS 3:1 Now the serpent was more subtle than any beast of the field which the Lord God had made. And he said unto the woman, Yea, hath God said, Ye shall not eat of every tree of the garden?

2 And the woman said unto the serpent, We may eat of the fruit of the trees of the garden:

3 But of the fruit of the tree which is in the midst of the garden, God hath said, Ye shall not eat of it, neither shall ye touch it, lest ye die.

4 And the serpent said unto the woman, Ye shall not surely die:

5 For God doth know that in the day ye eat thereof, then your eyes shall be opened, and ye shall be as gods, knowing good and evil.

6 And when the woman saw that the tree was good for food, and that it was pleasant to the eyes, and a tree to be desired to make one wise, she took of the fruit thereof, and did eat, and gave also unto her husband with her; and he did eat.

7 And the eyes of them both were opened, and they knew that they were naked; and they sewed fig leaves together, and made themselves aprons.

8 And they heard the voice of the Lord God walking in the garden in the cool of the day: and Adam and his wife hid themselves from the presence of the Lord God amongst the trees of the garden.

9 And the Lord God called unto Adam, and said unto him, Where art thou?

10 And he said, I heard thy voice in the garden, and I was afraid, because I was naked; and I hid myself.

11 And he said, Who told thee that thou wast naked? Hast thou eaten of the tree, whereof I commanded thee that thou shouldest not eat?

12 And the man said, The woman whom thou gavest to be with me, she gave me of the tree, and I did eat.

13 And the Lord God said unto the woman, What is this that thou hast done? And the woman said, The serpent beguiled me, and I did eat.

BIBLE BACKGROUND

Humankind was created male and female. Genesis 1:28 indicates that God gave both male and female responsibilities over His creation. They were to multiply and subdue the earth according to God's plan.

God gave Adam and Eve the gift of marriage. In the Garden of Eden, God caused the man to sleep, took a rib from the side of the man, and fashioned the woman from it. When Adam saw Eve, he immediately recognized her as an integral part of himself— "bone of my bones and flesh of my flesh" (Genesis 2:23). Genesis 2 ends with a profound statement: "And they were both naked, the man and his wife, and were not ashamed" (v. 25).

In the text we study today, our first parents are firmly established in the garden along with the other creatures God had made and Adam had named. One of these creatures plans to disrupt God's plan of tranquility and innocence for the human race.

POINTS TO PONDER

1. *What kind of creature was the serpent? (Genesis 3:1)*
2. *What did the serpent want to know from Eve? (v. 1)*
3. *How did the woman respond to the serpent? (vv. 2-3)*
4. *How did the serpent assure Eve that it would be correct for her and her husband to eat from the tree? (vv. 4-5)*
5. *What did Eve and Adam try to do once they found out they were naked? (vv. 7-8)*
6. *Who did Adam and Eve blame for their transgression? (vv. 12-13)*

LESSON AT-A-GLANCE

1. *Adam and Eve's encounter with the serpent (Genesis 3:1-7)*
2. *Adam and Eve's encounter with God (vv. 8-13)*

EXPLORING THE MEANING

1. Adam and Eve's encounter with the serpent (Genesis 3:1-7)

Genesis 3 begins with a different perspective from the first two chapters of the book. In the first two chapters, God's handiwork is seen as good and progressive. However, as we begin Chapter

3, there is a description of God's plan which had worldwide and eternal consequences.

The Bible doesn't specifically say where the serpent came from or what it was doing at the time it encountered Adam and Eve. But the Scriptures indicate that the serpent was made by God and it was "more cunning" than all the other beasts (v. 1, NKJV).

Ryrie states that in its uncursed state the serpent was a beautiful creature that probably did not crawl on the ground as serpents do today (*Ryrie Study Bible*, 1984, p. 11). Whether or not this is true we cannot really determine. But the serpent spoke to Eve probably in the same manner and tone as Adam had. The woman was not alarmed when the serpent talked with her, and, in her innocent state, she was not alarmed that creatures could talk.

The serpent asked her a question designed to get her to think about God's rule and authority: "Did God really say, 'You must not eat of any tree of the garden'?" (v. 1, NIV) The serpent's goal was twofold. First, he wanted to plant doubt in Eve's mind about God's goodness and fairness. Second, he wanted to see whether or not the woman would be obedient to God in the face of temptation.

Eve responded to the serpent's question by explaining to him the rules that God had given. God had placed both Adam and Eve in the Garden of Eden to care for it And He cared for them, providing food, companionship, and meaningful work. His only requirement was obedience.

There was one tree God specifically told Adam and Eve not to touch: the Tree of the Knowledge of Good and Evil. It was in the middle of the garden along with the Tree of Life (Genesis 2:9). If Adam and Eve touched or ate of that tree they would die—spiritually first, then physically. This statement implies that Adam and Eve were meant to live forever as the caretakers of God's earth.

Satan knew this. But he wanted to deceive the man and woman into forfeiting their control of earth.

The serpent told Eve that God was holding out on them, that He was depriving them of the right to be as God. The serpent said she and the man would not die if they ate of the Tree of the Knowledge of Good and Evil. Instead, their eyes would become open and they would be like God, knowing both good and evil (3:5).

Satan through the serpent used a good motive to tempt Eve to do wrong: "You shall be like God…" (v. 5). It wasn't wrong for Eve to want to be like God. That should always be our highest goal. But Satan misled Eve about how to accomplish this goal. He told her she could become more like God by defying God's authority, by taking God's place, by deciding for herself what was best for her life. In essence, Satan told Eve she could become her own god (*Amplified Bible*, 1988, p. 10).

Satan has told that same lie to countless millions of people throughout history, and we have paid a dear price for believing his deceptions. Self-exaltation leads to rebellion against God. As soon as we begin to disobey God, we place ourselves above God. This is what Satan enticed Adam and Eve to do.

Eve didn't hesitate to take the fruit from the tree and eat it. Plus, she wanted her husband to share in her experience. She gave Adam some of the fruit, and they both ate.

Satan's temptations are the same today. He tries to make us believe that sin is good, pleasant, and desirable. Often, our sins do not appear ugly to us, and the most attractive sins are the hardest to avoid.

Additionally, Eve involved her husband in her wrongdoing. That is one of the characteristics of sin. It spreads and affects many people—some who desperately try to avoid it. Why do we try to share our sin?

Once Adam and Eve ate fruit from the Tree of Knowledge of Good and Evil, their eyes became open. Suddenly they realized that they were naked and tried to hide their nakedness from each other by making coverings for themselves. The alarm of guilt and shame went off in their heads, and they tried to do something about it.

2. Adam and Eve's encounter with God (vv. 8-13)
Once sin came into the world, the man and woman's intimate relationship with God was severed. Their guilty feelings made them try to hide from God. How futile! Thank God we have a conscience too that goes off like an alarm when we do something wrong. Thank God also that we can quickly confess what we've done and receive forgiveness from God (1 John 1:9).

Someone has said that the thought of two human beings covered with fig leaves, trying to hide from the all-seeing, all-knowing God is humorous. While this may strike us as humorous, the reality is tragic. God called to Adam, asking where he was. God wanted the man and woman to "come clean."

The Scriptures do not say whether the man and woman came out of hiding, but they answered the Lord, admitting that they were naked and afraid. Because He is omniscient and omnipresent, God knew they had disobeyed Him by eating from the tree in the middle of the garden.

God wanted to hear from Adam, and Adam immediately laid the blame at his wife's feet (v. 12). His wife turned and blamed the serpent (v. 13). But how differently might the story have turned out had both Adam and Eve looked inwardly at what they had done?

How easy it is to excuse our sins by blaming someone else or circumstances. But God knows the truth and He holds each of us responsible for what we do. How refreshing it is to admit our wrong attitudes and actions and repent toward God. We still have to face the consequences of our sins, but what a wonderful assurance to have our guilt confessed and our sins forgiven! (Psalm 103:3)

DISCERNING MY DUTY

1. *Why did Satan use the serpent to do his work?*
2. *How do you think it was possible for the serpent to talk with the woman?*
3. *What kind of fruit did Adam and Eve eat?*
4. *Was it possible for Adam and Eve to hide from God? Why or why not?*
5. *Is it possible for us to hide from God? Why or why not?*

DECIDING MY RESPONSE

To think about—Our world is full of problems, including war in Europe, starvation in Africa, and racism in our own nation. These problems and many others are a result of sinful human beings who insist on disobeying God. If you were a Christian Secretary General presiding over the United Nations, list three or four ways you would go about solving these three problems.

To do—This week, examine your life to see whether or not you have tried to "hide" from God. Are there areas in your life you need to repent of and bring before the Lord? Spend time confessing your sins and asking God for cleansing and deliverance this week. Write down your thoughts and God's answers to your prayers in a journal, so you can review them during the week. Be sure to thank the Lord for answered prayer.

WHAT I WILL DO

LIGHT ON THE HEAVY

SERPENT. A reptile; in the Bible, another term for snake. In the ancient world, there was general respect for, revulsion at, and fear of serpents. Most were assumed to be poisonous and therefore dangerous. The serpent thus came to be understood symbolically with both positive and negative connotations. In some ancient cultures, the serpent was associated with deity and was depicted in statues and paintings with various gods and goddesses. Serpents also played various roles in ancient mythological stories. Some even linked the serpent with the process of healing, as in the case of the Greek god Asclepius. In Canaanite religion, which the early Hebrew people encountered upon their arrival in the area, the serpent was associated with the fertility worship of Baal, his consort Astarte being depicted with a serpent.

Against this general background, one is not surprised to find many references to serpents in biblical writings. In the Old Testament literature, serpents usually have a negative connotation. The story of creation recorded in Genesis 2:4-3:24, which explains the sinfulness of the human race, has as its villain the serpent. However, not until much later is the serpent in this story identified with Satan or the devil. In ancient mythology, particularly in Mesopotamia, the great sea serpent was another symbol for evil and chaos, the great enemy of order and the gods. In the Old Testament, references to Leviathan and Rahab (Job 26:12; Psalm 74:14; 104:26) are vestiges of this idea, and these creatures were understood to be the enemy of God and God's people. (*Harper's Bible Dictionary*, 1984, p. 928).

God Sets His People Free
Based on Exodus 6:2-9; 11:1-3; 12:21-36

DEFINING THE ISSUE

The Exodus story had great appeal for African slaves in the pre-Civil War South. Like the Israelites of old, they too found themselves a separated people, strangers in a foreign land, forced into inhumane bondage. The escape route to the North was called the Underground Railroad. The code name among the slaves for the Underground Railroad was "the business of Egypt." Escaping from slavery was called "getting out of Egypt," and the relative freedom of the North was referred to as the "Promised Land."

The most famous "conductor" of the Underground Railroad was a woman named Harriet Tubman, who was born a slave around 1823. Tubman, known as "The Black Moses," escaped from a Maryland plantation at the age of 25. She left behind her husband, parents, and brothers. But she was not satisfied with gaining freedom only for herself. Harriet Tubman made 19 trips back into the dangerous South, helping other slaves to escape. In all, she led more than 300 people to freedom, including her own parents.

This lesson details how God used Moses to free the children of Israel from the bondage of Egypt.

AIM

By the end of the lesson, students will understand there is a price to be paid for disobedience to God, clearly express how following the wrong people can lead to tragedy, and identify at least one area in their lives that they can bring into conformity to God's will.

SCRIPTURE TEXT

> EXODUS 6:5 And I have also heard the groaning of the children of Israel, whom the Egyptians keep in bondage; and I have remembered my covenant.
>
> 6 Wherefore say unto the children of Israel, I am the Lord, and I will bring you out from under the burdens of the Egyptians, and I will rid you out of their bondage, and I will redeem you with a stretched out arm, and with great judgments:
>
> 7 And I will take you to me for a people, and I will be to you a God: and ye shall know that I am the Lord your God, which bringeth you out from under the burdens of the Egyptians.
>
> 11:1 And the Lord said unto Moses, Yet will I bring one plague more upon Pharaoh, and upon Egypt; afterwards he will let you go hence: when he shall let you go, he shall surely thrust you out hence altogether.
>
> 12:29 And it came to pass, that at midnight the Lord smote all the firstborn in the land of Egypt, from the firstborn of Pharaoh that sat on his throne unto the firstborn of the captive that was in the dungeon; and all the firstborn of cattle.

30 And Pharaoh rose up in the night, he, and all his servants, and all the Egyptians; and there was a great cry in Egypt; for there was not a house where there was not one dead.

31 And he called for Moses and Aaron by night, and said, Rise up, and get you forth from among my people, both ye and the children of Israel; and go, serve the Lord, as ye have said.

32 Also take your flocks and your herds, as ye have said, and be gone; and bless me also.

33 And the Egyptians were urgent upon the people, that they might send them out of the land in haste; for they said, We be all dead men.

BACKGROUND

In the previous study, we took note of how God revealed Himself to Moses by His sacred name, Jehovah, and sent him back to Egypt. God commanded Moses to go to the king of Egypt and request that the Israelites be allowed to go into the desert and worship. But before going to Pharaoh, Moses had to first gain the confidence of his own people.

Aaron, Moses's brother, told the people all the things God had revealed. Moses then verified the words of Aaron through miraculous signs which caused the people to believe (4:30-31).

Moses was now ready to begin his mission to Pharaoh. He and Aaron went to Pharaoh and asked permission to go into the desert and worship God. Pharaoh responded by charging Moses with keeping the people from their work, and ordered additional work to prevent any further demands. He commanded that no straw be given to the Israelites to make bricks.

The events of Exodus 5 mark the lowest and most hopeless period in the entire 430-year history of the Israelites in Egypt. In their frustration they directed their anger at Moses. And even Moses was ready to give up after the disastrous results of his encounter with Pharaoh.

POINTS TO PONDER

1. *When Moses originally went to Pharaoh, he requested that the Israelites be allowed to go into the desert to worship God. What was Pharaoh's response to this request? (Exodus 5:4, 7)*

2. *Why did God stress that He would be the one to bring the people out of bondage? (6:6)*

3. *What is the ancient meaning of the word "redeem"? Who was responsible for redeeming a person from slavery? (v. 6)*

4. *When God told Moses about the final plague He would bring on Egypt, He gave him a guarantee. What was the guarantee? (11:1)*

5. *At what time did the last plague occur, and who was killed? (12:29)*

6. *Why were the Egyptians in such a hurry for the Israelites to finally leave Egypt? (v. 33)*

LESSON AT-A-GLANCE

1. *God announces His deliverance (Exodus 6:5-7)*
2. *God announces His judgment (11:1)*
3. *God cancels life for the firstborn (12:29-33)*

EXPLORING THE MEANING

1. God announces His deliverance (Exodus 6:5-7)

Many situations don't work out the way we think they should. Often when this happens we become despondent and wonder where God is in all of this. But usually it is in our darkest moments, when all hope appears lost, that God reveals Himself as our deliverer. Moses had reached that point. He had done everything God commanded, and it appeared God had let him down.

God encouraged Moses by reminding him that He is not some far off, impersonal God, but is involved personally and intimately in the affairs of His people. God reminded Moses of who He is (6:2-4): Jehovah is God's covenant name. The self-existent Creator revealed Himself to His covenant people as the unchanging God who remains faithful to all promises. He linked their coming deliverance to the promise that He had made to Abraham (Genesis 15:18) to give his descendants the land of Canaan (Exodus 4). He assured Moses that He had heard their cries of bondage (v. 5a) and was aware of His promise (v. 5b).

In verses 6-8, God announces to Moses His sevenfold plan of redemption:

1. *"I will bring you out from under the burdens of the Egyptians" (v. 6):* Redemption is not achieved through human efforts. God, and God alone, makes us free. God is the source of our redemption.

2. *"I will rid you out of their bondage" (v. 6):* The word "rid" comes from a Hebrew word meaning to "snatch away." At a time of God's choosing, the Israelites would suddenly be snatched from slavery and set free. The same is true for us in the spiritual realm. Once we yield to God, He snatches

us out of the kingdom of darkness and places us into the kingdom of His dear Son (Colossians 1:13).

3. *"I will redeem you with a stretched out arm" (v. 6):* In ancient times, to redeem meant to buy back the freedom of a person who had been sold into slavery. The redemptive responsibility belonged to that person's nearest living relative. This relative was known as the kinsman redeemer. God is saying to the children of Israel that He is their kinsman redeemer, and it is His responsibility to bring about their freedom.

    God promised to bring about their freedom with an outstretched arm. He would stretch out His arm until it reached a predetermined goal. God's purpose was not simply to set His people free, but to fulfill His promise to Abraham that all the nations in the earth would be blessed through his seed (Genesis 22:18).

    The first three *"I will"* statements of Exodus 6 deal with the actual physical deliverance of the Israelites from slavery. The next four statements are promises of God's care after their deliverance.

4. *"I will take you to me for a people" (v.7a):* An old gospel song says, "God didn't bring us this far to leave us." God did not simply free the children of Israel to leave them alone. He chose them as people dedicated to Himself, and He dwelt among them. Likewise, He did not free us from the bondage of sin simply to get us out of hell and into heaven, but also to "get God into us."

5. *"I will be to you a God" (v. 7):* What an awesome statement this is! The people who were once slaves to men are to become the children of God. Some time in eternity past, God chose the tiny nation of Israel to be a people set apart

for Himself. This choice was not based on merit, but on the all-knowing purposes of God. None of us is worthy of God's divine adoption. God did not single us out because we are somehow special. No, we are special because God singled us out. The reason for God's choice is His pleasure (Ephesians 1:4-5).

6. *"I will bring you in unto the land" (v. 8a):* The land is Canaan, the same land that God promised Abraham hundreds of years before. Some commenters regard Canaan as a picture of the Christian life. We believers have been delivered from the rule of Satan, and we have become rulers through our union with Christ (Ephesians 2:6). Our citizenship in heaven is not just a future promise, but a current spiritual reality (Philippians 3:20).

7. *"I will give you [the land] for an heritage" (v. 8b):* God would bring the Israelites into the new land, but He also promised it to them as an eternal inheritance. When God freed us from the bondage of sin, He also gave us the gift of eternal life with Him, our inheritance.

2. God announces His judgment (11:1)

Redemption and judgment are like two sides of the same coin. Redemption is promised to everyone who hears and obeys, while judgment is the cost of disobedience.

God gave Pharaoh many opportunities to obey His word. In chapters 7-10, Moses goes to Pharaoh several times with God's command, "Let my people go." Each time Pharaoh refuses to obey the Word of God. After each refusal, God executes His judgment on Egypt through increasingly harsh calamities.

Pharaoh responds to God's judgments by hardening his heart or having God harden it for him. The Bible uses two different

Hebrew words to describe the hardening of Pharaoh's heart. When Pharaoh hardens his own heart, the word used is *kobed*, which means oppressive or harsh. When God hardens Pharaoh's heart, the word is *chazaq*, which means to strengthen. God was not the cause of Pharaoh's stubbornness; He simply made evident what was already the state of Pharaoh's heart. The plagues were intended to force Pharaoh to recognize that God is supreme and should be obeyed, to demonstrate to Israel the power of their God, and to execute judgment on Egypt and their gods. The 10 plagues touched every phase of Egyptian life: animal, vegetable, and human. Yet Pharaoh still refused to obey God—until the last and most devastating plague, which comes with a guarantee: not only will Pharaoh allow the Israelites to leave, but he will drive them out (11:1).

3. God cancels life for the firstborn (12:29-33)

Sin is rebellion or disobedience to the will of God. Sometimes misfortunes are God's way of reaching people. Such was the case with Pharaoh. Ten times God commanded Pharaoh to yield. Ten times he refused.

Chapter 12 is the high point of the Exodus story. The chapter opens with God instituting the Passover as a memorial celebrating Israel's deliverance from Egypt (vv. 1-20). God instructs Moses and Aaron about the preparations the Israelites must make to protect themselves from the final horror. Every household was to kill a lamb. The blood of that lamb was to be collected in bowls and smeared over the doorposts of their homes. When the Lord sent the Death Angel through Egypt and executed His divine judgment, He would see the blood on the doorpost and pass by their homes (vv. 21-23).

At midnight the Lord's angel struck. The firstborn of every family in Egypt died. There were no exceptions. Everyone from Pharaoh's heir to the son of the prisoner in the dungeon killed. The firstborn of all the animals in Egypt also died. There was not one house among all Egyptians that was spared (vv. 29-30). Pharaoh was beaten. That very night he sent for Moses and ordered the Israelites to leave Egypt immediately. The Egyptian people urged the Israelites to hurry because they too had learned to fear God. They believed that He would kill them all if the Israelites delayed (vv. 31-33).

Time after time, God gave Pharaoh the opportunity to turn away from his disobedience. If Pharaoh had obeyed, he could have spared his people their agony.

The death and blood of the sacrificial lamb was a symbolic offering. In Old Testament times, God accepted animal sacrifices in place of the life of the sinner. When Jesus came, He became our Sacrificial Lamb. His blood freed us from both the bondage and the penalty of sin. Our part is to turn away from our rebellion and surrender our lives to Him.

DISCERNING MY DUTY

1. *Why is it that redemption and judgment seem to go hand-in-hand?*
2. *Did God cause Pharaoh to be disobedient by hardening his heart?*
3. *Why didn't God begin the conflict with Egypt by killing the firstborn of Egypt, sparing them the other nine plagues?*
4. *The Israelites were saved from death by the Lord when He saw the blood of a spotless lamb painted above their doors. What does this symbolize for believers today?*

DECIDING MY RESPONSE

To think about—1. God gave Egypt many signs of His displeasure before executing His final judgment on the land. As you look around your city and our country, do you see any signs of God's displeasure?

2. The nation of Egypt suffered because of the willful disobedience and arrogance of its leaders. What are some ways the leaders of our nation are disobedient to God?

3. What effect do you think it would have on our country if we elected leaders who were concerned about pleasing God? Do you take a politician's spiritual values into consideration when you vote?

To do—Spend some time this week examining your life for areas or relationships where you may be disobedient to God's will. List those areas on a sheet of paper and refer to them during your prayer time. Make a daily habit of confessing these areas to God and asking His forgiveness and deliverance. Refer to your list at the beginning of each day and determine with God's help to bring these areas into accordance with His will.

WHAT I WILL DO

___
___
___
___
___
___
___

LIGHT ON THE HEAVY

God's Plagues on Egypt:

1. The first plague of bloody waters was directed against Osiris, the god of the Nile.
2. The second plague of frogs was against the frog goddess Hekt.
3. The third plague of lice was against Seb, the earth god.
4. The fourth plague of beetles (or flies) was against Hatkok, the wife of Osiris.
5. The fifth plague of cattle disease was against Apis, the sacred bull god.
6. The sixth plague, boils, was against Typhon.
7. The seventh plague, hail and fire, was against Shu, the god of the atmosphere.
8. The eighth plague, locusts, was against Serapia, the god who protected Egypt against locusts.
9. The ninth plague, darkness, was against Ra, the sun god.
10. The tenth plague, the death of the firstborn, was an attack on all gods.

(Dr. H. L. Wilmington, *Wilmington's Guide to the Bible*, Wheaton, IL: Tyndale House, pp. 66-67.)

God Covenants with His People
Based on Exodus 19:4-6; 20:1-17

DEFINING THE ISSUE

The room was thick and tense with silence. A dozen people sat in folding chairs, nervous, tired, and...hopeful. These were drug addicts who had heard the Gospel through Urbanline, a group of Christian ex-addicts who shared Christ with addicts on the street. The program was tough. Michael Johnson, the director, explained the program to the group.

"We have a 90% success rate here at Urbanline. That's because we recognize that the best way to deal with an addiction is to replace it with the ultimate addiction: Jesus Christ. The Lord Jesus Christ will become your 'fix.' Television viewing is monitored to discourage temptation through the images portrayed. Every day is Sunday...we start the day with Bible study and prayer. We are praying for you and with you all day, and we end the day with Bible study and prayer. Old habits like lying, stealing, and accusing each other will go out the window. These were tactics for getting drugs. Some of you even used your wives, girlfriends, and children to supply your habits." Heads hung low.

"You have made a commitment to Jesus Christ...a covenant... that involves your life. You were slaves to powders and crystals. Christ has set you free. But even freedom has conditions. There are things you must do to stay free. If anyone has a problem with any of this, he is free to go." There were sighs and shuffling of feet. Tears stung the eyes of Carl Smith as he fought to keep from running out of the room.

Michael continued, "I suppose the question is, will you be a slave to drugs or a son of the King?" Carl relaxed and wiped the tears away. He would be a son of the King.

AIM

By the end of the lesson, students will refamiliarize themselves with the Ten Commandments, a covenant summed up by our Lord Jesus Christ in two new commandments: love God and love your neighbor. Students will also use the coming week as Ten Commandments Awareness Week, taking note of two things: 1) how well they keep the commandments and 2) how our society is affected by the keeping or breaking of the Ten Commandments.

SCRIPTURE TEXT

> EXODUS 19:4 Ye have seen what I did unto the Egyptians, and how I bare you on eagles' wings, and brought you unto myself.
>
> 5 Now therefore, if ye will obey my voice indeed, and keep my covenant, then ye shall be a peculiar treasure unto me above all people: for all the earth is mine:
>
> 6 And ye shall be unto me a kingdom of priests, and an holy nation. These are the words which thou shalt speak unto the children of Israel.
>
> 20:2 I am the Lord thy God, which have brought thee out of the land of Egypt, out of the house of bondage.

3 Thou shalt have no other gods before me.

4 Thou shalt not make unto thee any graven image, or any likeness of any thing that is in heaven above, or that is in the earth beneath, or that is in the water under the earth:

7 Thou shalt not take the name of the Lord thy God in vain; for the Lord will not hold him guiltless that taketh his name in vain.

8 Remember the sabbath day, to keep it holy.

9 Six days shalt thou labour, and do all thy work:

10 But the seventh day is the sabbath of the Lord thy God: in it thou shalt not do any work, thou, nor thy son, nor thy daughter, thy manservant, nor thy maidservant, nor thy cattle, nor thy stranger that is within thy gates:

11 For in six days the Lord made heaven and earth, the sea, and all that in them is, and rested the seventh day: wherefore the Lord blessed the sabbath day, and hallowed it.

12 Honour thy father and thy mother: that thy days may be long upon the land which the Lord thy God giveth thee.

13 Thou shalt not kill.

14 Thou shalt not commit adultery.

15 Thou shalt not steal.

16 Thou shalt not bear false witness against thy neighbour.

17 Thou shalt not covet thy neighbour's house, thou shalt not covet thy neighbour's wife, nor his manservant, nor his maidservant, nor his ox, nor his ass, nor any thing that is thy neighbour's.

BIBLE BACKGROUND

The Hebrews had been free from their Egyptian slave masters for roughly three months. They were encamped in the Sinai desert in front of Mount Horeb. Moses had gone up the mountain at God's command to receive instructions for these people who were destined to be God's special treasure. The laws received by Moses for the Hebrews would accomplish three things: reverse the effects of slavery; nullify the impact of 430 years of Egyptian religion, customs, traditions, and government; and prepare the people to be a unique nation whose King would be God.

The most memorable of all the laws and ordinances are what we know as the "Ten Commandments," upon which hang the justice systems of many countries of the world.

POINTS TO PONDER

1. *Which three commandments defined God's relationship with His people? (Exodus 20:3-7)*
2. *What two things did God do to the Sabbath? (20:11)*
3. *Which six commandments define our relationships with each other? (20:12-17)*
4. *Which commandment had a promise attached? (20:12)*
5. *List six specific things we should not covet. (20:17)*

THE UNFOLDING STORY OF GOD'S SALVATION PLAN

LESSON AT-A-GLANCE

1. *The God of the covenant (Exodus 19:4)*
2. *The people of the covenant (19:5)*
3. *The goal of the covenant (19:6)*
4. *The covenant (20:2-17)*
   A. *With respect to God—the fear clause (20:2-7)*
   B. *With respect to self—the faith clause (20:8-11)*
   C. *With respect to each other—the love clause (20:12-17)*

EXPLORING THE MEANING

1. The God of the covenant (Exodus 19:4)

With the phrase, "Ye have seen what I did unto the Egyptians," God announces Himself to be the exclusive God of the people of Israel. With the miracles inflicted by His awesome power, God not only freed the Israelites, He brought judgment on the gods of the Egyptians. Each plague was a direct attack on a specific Egyptian deity. Israel's God proved Himself infinitely more powerful than any magic or false gods.

God set about to undo 430 years of Egyptian culture (religion, politics, economics), as well as to reverse the effects of slavery, including fear of failure and dependence on an oppressor. He required Israel's undivided loyalty and gave them regulations for maintaining this covenant relationship (Judaism), a government (theocracy), and an economic system (giving and forgiving).

2. The people of the covenant (19:5)

God gave His people one stipulation: obey. He did not require that they do great feats, go beyond their capabilities, or make unreasonable sacrifices like sacrificing their children on altars. He simply insisted that they obey His voice. Why? If they were not willing to obey His voice, how would He provide for, protect, lead, and bless them? These benefits were all a part of the covenant—His agreement with them.

The Christian liberty we enjoy in Christ Jesus also involves our obedience. If we do not obey the Word of God, we suffer the natural and spiritual consequences of disobedience. The kind of life we lead is a reflection of the level of our commitment to Christ and His New Covenant.

3. The goal of the covenant (19:6)
The goal of the covenant was to make Israel a nation unlike any other, a nation whose King was God—a theocracy. Israel's religion would not be based on shedding blood in sacrifices to gods. Israel's economic stability and prosperity would not be based on preying on other nations. Their system of giving tithes and offerings would ensure that everyone was taken care of. Forgiveness and abundant blessings were the benefits they would receive for obeying and honoring the God of the covenant.

4. The covenant (20:2-17)
A. *With respect to God—the fear clause (20:2-7)*

The first three commandments would ensure that the people of Israel would be different from other nations.

They were prohibited from worshiping any other gods. Other nations had few problems with "mixing and matching" gods. Other nations often worshiped many gods. In Egypt, for example, almost everything in nature was worshiped as a god—even flies! The Hebrews would worship ONE God who was greater than all the others (vv. 3-4).

Further, they would not be allowed to create images of their God. To do so would bring Him down from His rightfully exalted position. Images would confine God, who is Spirit, to space, and eventually confine Him to their own perceptions and private interpretations of Him. If a physical image of God could be formed by their own imaginations and hands, sooner or later they would do the same to the very character and nature of God distorting Him and reducing Him to a deity who could be carved, fashioned, and manipulated. They might even convince themselves that He had given permission to practice the perversions of other cultures. The second commandment is a reminder that God alone is the Creator and we are His creatures.

Our God is a jealous God. The consequences of His jealousy, provoked by disobedience to these commands, are felt by future generations. On the other hand, He shows mercy to those who love and obey Him.

In the third commandment, God demands from His people reverence for His very name. Others, frequently without thought, invoked the names of their gods in even the most trivial matters of conversation. This would not be so in Israel.

These three commandments can be called the "fear clause," a reminder of an awesome God who deserves reverence and respect, a God whose authority should not be challenged.

B. *With respect to self—the faith clause (20:8-11)*

Of the seven days of the week, one day was to be a day of rest from all labor. God initiated this day of rest when He rested or stood back from His own works (Genesis 2:2-3).

What were the purpose and benefits of the Sabbath? First, there was the obvious need to rest physically, so that the body could be refreshed and renewed. The Lord wanted the Israelites to be a robust and vigorous people. Second, slaves do not have "off days." They are on duty at all times. The Israelites were no longer slaves. This day of rest would be one of God's methods of reversing the effects of slavery. Only the free could afford time off. Next, the Sabbath would serve as a reminder of their dependence on God, who had provided for them and continued to do so even as they rested from their labors (Exodus 16:22-30). Finally, the Sabbath would provide a day for the people to reflect upon their God, to be grateful to Him for all He had done, to come together to worship Him and thank Him for His continuing mercy and blessings.

This was the "faith clause," which encouraged Israel to continue believing in God's ability and willingness to protect and provide. They would continue to be sustained, but not based on their own works.

C. *With respect to each other—the love clause (20:12-17)*

The last six commandments of the covenant are meant to foster unity and community among the people—starting with the family. Children are encouraged to honor their parents. This is the only commandment with a promise attached. The New Testament states that long life is promised, and that life would "go well" with obedient children (Ephesians 6:2-3, NIV). Of course, this could be taken literally since there were laws calling for the stoning of insubordinate children. But the promised blessing was also social and spiritual because an obedient child would most likely become a cooperative, pleasant, law-abiding adult.

Murder, the intentional taking of innocent life, is prohibited. Hence, captured in this commandment is the premise that human life is precious. If people are permitted to kill at will, soon there will be no people. We need to give serious thought to the rate at which violence in our "modern and enlightened" society is reducing our population—particularly the young, African American male population.

Adultery is forbidden. Marriage is a covenant instituted by God. Adultery severely damages and/or nullifies that covenant. Adultery not only disrupts the covenant between marriage partners, but also affects family unity so that it cannot effectively carry out God's plans and purposes.

Stealing is not only wrong but unnecessary in God's "perfect" society where one serves the Lord who provides for His people and blesses them abundantly. To steal is, in effect, to accuse God of failing to provide for His own. In fact, stealing is merely an expression of one's own innate greed, ingratitude, and discontent with what God has provided. It also shows an attitude of not caring for one's neighbor and not respecting that neighbor's possessions.

One sure way to disrupt the unity of community life is to lie to and about each other. Since trust in any context is based on truth, when truth is absent, trust becomes impossible. When one cannot trust one's neighbor, suspicion settles in. If we cannot trust those we see every day then how will we fully trust God whom we cannot see? If we lie to each other, what will prevent us from lying to God?

Lastly, the Israelites are commanded not to **covet** or lust for the possessions of other people. While God's chosen people would be a blessed and prosperous people if they obeyed the Lord, there was no promise of the equal distribution of wealth. Some would possess more than others. Those possessing less wealth might be tempted to want what their neighbors had, and, unchecked, these intense desires could lead to hostilities and acts of stealing, lying, and even murder. On the other hand, those possessing more could be filled with greed and want to have the meager possessions of the poor.

And so, we see that the Ten Commandments are not simply a childhood recitation, but a serious, abiding covenant in ten parts designed to shape a meaningful, caring, free society for those who would choose to live by that covenant. These commandments are God-given, ageless, and timeless—working as well in today's society as in the Israelite camp of over 4,000 years ago.

DISCERNING MY DUTY

1. *Why do you think God started out with just ten basic laws for His people?*
2. *How could these laws help the Israelites experience a sense of community?*
3. *Why did God begin by reminding the people of what He had done for them?*
4. *What do you think was the significance of the first three commandments? Could God have added other commandments concerning Himself? Give an example.*
5. *How could the last six commandments provide a good foundation, even for a non-Christian society?*

DECIDING MY RESPONSE

To think about—1. Is it still possible to live our lives by the Ten Commandments? Why or why not?

2. If you could pick only one commandment to address the issue of gang violence, which would you choose and why?

3. As society worsens, more laws are being passed to deal with its immorality. Is it possible to "legislate" morality? Explain.

To do—Read the Ten Commandments in Exodus 20:3-17. Why not make this Ten Commandments Awareness Week? Be aware of how well you keep the Ten Commandments. Are you taking the Lord's name in vain ("Oh, Lord!" "Jesus Christ!" "Lordy, Lordy!")? While most Christians do not use profanity habitually, sometimes things come out of our mouths which shouldn't. And sometimes we wish we could have Brother Rich's BMW. When was the last time your response to a phone call was, "Tell them I'm not in"? Share with the class next week the results of Ten Commandments Awareness Week—and maybe have a few chuckles as well.

WHAT I WILL DO

_____
_____
_____
_____

LIGHT ON THE HEAVY

COVENANT—Covenant is not an everyday term in modern society; "contract" is a more common substitute. What's the difference? In biblical use, "covenant" differs from a contract in two ways. First, a covenant has no termination date, whereas a contract always does. Second, a covenant applies to the whole of a person, whereas a contract involves only a part, especially a skill possessed by a person or a service to be rendered. In the Old Testament, the Hebrew word *berith* is translated as covenant, and comes from a root which means "to cut." This refers to the cutting or dividing of animals into two parts. The two parties of the covenant pass between them in making the covenant affirming, "May the Lord split me into like this animal if I fail to keep my word." (*Dictionary of the Bible*, Carmel, Guideposts)

What Do These Stones Mean?
Based on Joshua 4:1-3, 8-24

DEFINING THE ISSUE

What is it about memorials that are so special? Why do people attach a certain significance to memorials? Just the other day, a four-year-old girl was sitting in a shopping cart in a department store. The child was sobbing terribly because her mother wanted to buy some music for her husband's birthday. The child hollered, "We ALWAYS buy Daddy socks and ties for his birthday!" It doesn't take long for an object to become attached to a memory!

We often mark special events in specific ways. Perhaps we put up a Christmas tree to celebrate Christmas. Or we mark a loved one's grave site with a tombstone. We celebrate birthdays, anniversaries, and achievements with gifts, cards, and flowers, so the recipient of the gift will not forget our gesture of honoring him or her!

God has given us an opportunity to memorialize the occasion of salvation when He sent Jesus into the world. When the right time came about, God sent His Son to be born of a woman to redeem us that we might become part of His family (see Galatians 4:4-5). When it was the right time, God "marked" His plan of salvation by His Son's death on the cross, and His resurrection from the grave. God encourages us to commemorate those special occasions (Luke 22:19).

This study will allow us to see how God moved on behalf of His people and commanded them to memorialize His mighty actions that future generations would not forget how He provided for them in their time of need.

This is an important lesson. When God is gracious to answer prayers for our family, do we share what He has done with others? Do we make sure that even our little ones know what He has done in our lives? By acknowledging Him with praise and thanksgiving, we are showing Him we appreciate what He has done. We also show others that we have not forgotten His past blessings.

AIM

Students will learn the importance of memorial events and incorporate them in their own lives as they worship God.

SCRIPTURE TEXT

> JOSHUA 4:1 And it came to pass, when all the people were clean passed over Jordan, that the Lord spake unto Joshua, saying,
>
> 2 Take you twelve men out of the people, out of every tribe a man,
>
> 3 And command ye them, saying, Take you hence out of the midst of Jordan, out of the place where the priests' feet stood firm, twelve stones, and ye shall carry them over with you, and leave them in the lodging place, where ye shall lodge this night.

8 And the children of Israel did so as Joshua commanded, and took up twelve stones out of the midst of Jordan, as the Lord spake unto Joshua, according to the number of the tribes of the children of Israel, and carried them over with them unto the place where they lodged, and laid them down there.

15 And the Lord spake unto Joshua, saying,

16 Command the priests that bear the ark of the testimony, that they come up out of Jordan.

17 Joshua therefore commanded the priests, saying, Come ye up out of Jordan.

18 And it came to pass, when the priests that bare the ark of the covenant of the Lord were come up out of the midst of Jordan, and the soles of the priests' feet were lifted up unto the dry land, that the waters of Jordan returned unto their place, and flowed over all his banks, as they did before.

19 And the people came up out of Jordan on the tenth day of the first month, and encamped in Gilgal, in the east border of Jericho.

20 And those twelve stones, which they took out of Jordan, did Joshua pitch in Gilgal.

21 And he spake unto the children of Israel, saying, When your children shall ask their fathers in time to come, saying, What mean these stones?

22 Then ye shall let your children know, saying, Israel came over this Jordan on dry land.

23 For the Lord your God dried up the waters of Jordan from before you, until ye were passed over, as the Lord your God did to the Red sea, which he dried up from before us, until we were gone over:

24 That all the people of the earth might know the hand of the Lord, that it is mighty: that ye might fear the Lord your God for ever.

BIBLE BACKGROUND

Joshua was born in Egypt and worked with Moses as his right-hand man during the Jewish exodus and wandering in the desert. He was also with Moses as an attendant in Mount Sinai when the rebellious people made a golden calf while Moses was on the mountain (Exodus 32:1-12).

When God spoke face-to-face with Moses in the tent, Joshua was there (Exodus 33:11). Joshua, along with Caleb, was a faithful spy in Canaan who declared the people should go in and possess the land as God had directed. For their faithfulness and loyalty, God kept both Joshua and Caleb alive so they could reach the Promised Land. Moses himself had designated Joshua as his successor and publicly had him installed (Deuteronomy 1:31; 31:14, 23).

The Book of Joshua is considered the first one of the former prophets in Hebrew, possibly because it is a teaching book showing how God's message was carried among the Jewish people. Joshua is closely connected to the Pentateuch (Genesis through Deuteronomy), and the six books together are called the Hexateuch.

The Book of Joshua records the taking of the Promised Land. It is broken into three sections: the conquest of Canaan (chapters 1-12), the distribution of the land (chapters 13-22), and Joshua's final address and death (chapters 23-24).

The ark of the covenant carried by the priests through the Jordan River was often called the ark of the testimony. God had given Moses the Law on stone tablets (Exodus 31:18) and had given detailed instructions about the chest He wanted built to hold it (see Exodus 25:10-22). Priests from the tribe of Levi were entrusted with the care of this ark. Not only did this chest contain the testimony, but it was here that Jehovah received from the high priest the atoning sacrifice for the sins of the people. Imagine the sense of great awe which the people must have felt during this experience!

In this lesson, Joshua is leading his people in the springtime when the River Jordan was swollen with melted snow. Some speculate that God caused a blockage and dammed the river. This helped the people cross over the river with the priests leading the way with the ark of the covenant. The Bible also says that "all of Israel crossed over on dry ground, until all the people had crossed completely over the Jordan" (Joshua 3:17, NKJV).

POINTS TO PONDER

1. *Who told Joshua to take the stones from the Jordan River? (Joshua 4:1-3)*
2. *What did the 12 stones represent? (4:8)*
3. *Who were the last people to cross the river? (4:18)*
4. *When did the waters rush back into place? (4:18-19)*
5. *What were parents supposed to teach their children? (4:22-24)*

LESSON AT-A-GLANCE

1. *The people cross over the Jordan (Joshua 4:1-3)*
2. *The people obey Joshua (v. 8)*

3. The people memorialize the event (vv. 15-24)
   A. And the priests come up from the Jordan (vv. 15-18)
   B. And they set up the stones at Gilgal (vv. 19-22)
   C. And are reminded of God's miracle (vv. 23, 24)

EXPLORING THE MEANING

1. The people cross over the Jordan (Joshua 4:1-3)

The Jordan River is a deep, narrow, and muddy river that rushes powerfully. Only a bridge or a miracle of God could provide a safe crossing.

God had already instructed Joshua on how to lead the people over the Jordan (see Joshua 3:1-17). God also instructed Joshua to select one man from each of the 12 tribes to take a stone out of the water and carry it with them. They were to carry the stones to the place where they would lodge that night (see 4:19).

Sometimes we don't understand why God directs our lives the way He does. But the Bible says, "'My thoughts are not your thoughts, neither are your ways my ways,' declares the Lord. 'As the heavens are higher than the earth, so are my ways higher than your ways and my thoughts than your thoughts'" (Isaiah 55:8-9, NIV). When God gives us direction, we shouldn't question Him. We should just obey!

2. The people obey Joshua (v. 8)

After the 12 men picked up the stones from the Jordan, they may have asked Joshua, "Why did we need to pick up these stones?" Joshua told the people what the stones meant. They were to be a memorial to the children of Israel showing how God had performed a miracle by holding back the waters of the Jordan (v. 7). The people obeyed Joshua and brought the stones with them to Gilgal and laid them down as a monument before the Lord.

Have you ever built a "monument" before the Lord? It may mean that you have a family altar in your home where you go to pray and meditate every day. Or it could be a place where you reverence the Lord for His great blessings to you. What is most important, however, is that we are consistent with our praise and thanksgiving. Too many of us are "hit-and-miss" Christians. We "hit" a week in our prayer life, and "miss" a week. However, if we purpose in our hearts to meet God at our family altar or our "monument," God will reveal Himself to us in a very real way. Let's remember that God is a Spirit and we need to worship Him in spirit and truth (see John 4:24).

3. The people memorialize the event (vv. 15-24)

A. *And the priests come up from the Jordan (vv. 15-18)*

It must have been a great scene to see 40,000 people passing over the Jordan River without even getting wet (see 4:10-13). Once they crossed over, the Bible says that the Lord magnified Joshua in the sight of all Israel, so that they feared him just as they feared Moses.

The last to cross over were the priests who bore the ark of the testimony. God told Joshua to command them to come out of the Jordan. This would identify Joshua as the supreme authority in Israel. Until the ark had crossed safely, the crossing was not complete. Therefore, when the ark made it to dry ground, and the soles of the priests' feet touched the land, the waters of the Jordan returned to where they had been, and the river continued to flow.

God showed the people that He was in control although He used Joshua as His vessel. Even today, God uses human vessels to do His work and to lead His people. When God's glory rests upon His servants, they have God's anointing and power to do His work; but we need to realize that it is God who is working through people to get the job done!

B. *And they set up the stones at Gilgal (vv. 19-22)*

The people came up out of the Jordan River on the tenth day of the first month. The tenth day was four days before Passover. So selecting a lamb for the Passover would have been an additional reason for rejoicing at that time.

The people camped in Gilgal, on the east border of Jericho. Gilgal was about five miles from the river and continued to be a meeting place for the people years afterward. In Gilgal, the 12 men who took the stones out of the Jordan set them up as a monument, as Joshua had instructed.

After the stones were set up, Joshua gathered all the people around the monument. They probably wondered why Joshua was so concerned about these stones. However, Joshua assured the people that the monument was special. "When your children ask their fathers in time to come, saying, 'What are these stones?' Then you shall let your children know, saying, Israel crossed over this Jordan on dry land" (vv. 21-22).

C. *And are reminded of God's miracles (vv. 23-24)*

Joshua reminded the people that it was God who dried up the waters of the Jordan just as He had dried up the Red Sea. God's hand was moving on their behalf. His miracles were still available for them, even though Moses was no longer leading them. The people were to build this monument in memory of God's deliverance. Joshua, the Lord's spokesman, made it clear that they were to acknowledge

His presence in their lives, not only for themselves but also for all the peoples of the earth to see. More important, the monument was to be built so that they could tell their children of the wonderful works of the Lord and honor Him for His great works.

Too many times, parents assume that their children will learn the ways of the Lord just by growing up in a home where prayers are said occasionally and going to church is taken very lightly. Some parents believe that because they are sincere Christians, their children will be. However, it is more important that children be taught the ways of the Lord and be led to Him so they can become saved. Otherwise, the world and its system will devour them because parents were not diligent in doing what was necessary for their child. Even in the Old Testament times children asked their parents hundreds of questions, such as "What is this?" and "What is the meaning of that?" Joshua instructed the parents to have a ready explanation for their children, giving glory and praises to God for His marvelous provisions. The stones would arouse the curiosity of many heathen nations and would serve as a testimony for them. The stones would stimulate the telling of the true story to share the goodness, mercy, and power of God. For some, the monument would become a casual part of the scenery. For others, the structure would increase their faith and appreciation of God.

What helps us remember and memorialize our relationship with Christ? It is the communion service which memorializes the blood shed on the cross for our sins. Through this ceremony we remember the love of God for us. We need to remember how much the Father loves us so that we may share that love with others.

DISCERNING MY DUTY

1. How does Scripture show that Joshua was given authority by God?
2. Why is it important for people to remember special events?
3. Why must parents pass traditions along to their children?
4. Should parents leave the teachings of the things of the Lord to the church? Why or why not? Where should most of the teachings come from?

DECIDING MY RESPONSE

1. Set aside a period of time to recall blessings of your past and thank God for these. Perhaps you can make a list of significant events and hang it where you will see it at the start or end of each day. You may want to build a small family altar nearby with memorial events displayed. Photographs and small objects can also help you.
2. Talk with a child who is a willing listener, telling of answered prayer in your life. Be specific. Recall instances of your personal family history. Faith is built by hearing testimonies of God's blessings in others' lives.

WHAT I WILL DO

_____
_____
_____
_____
_____
_____
_____

LIGHT ON THE HEAVY

LEVITES. The tribe of Levi was charged with caring for and transporting the sanctuary and all the materials used for elaborate worship services. They were descendants of Levi, son of Jacob. One of the reasons this tribe was chosen for this service is because they were the only tribe to voluntarily renounce the golden calf and show zeal for God's honor (see Exodus 32:1-26).

ACACIA TREE. Shittah tree was another name for this tree which grew in the Jordan Valley from the Sea of Galilee to the Dead Sea. Its strong, durable wood was largely used in the woodwork of the ark, the tabernacle itself, and furnishings in the tabernacle.

GILGAL. Gilgal was the first camp the Israelites set up after crossing the Jordan River and the location of a memorial made from stones taken from the riverbed. Because the river was so muddy and rough, such stones would have attracted attention. Also, Gilgal was the headquarters for the Israelites while they fought to conquer Canaan. (*New Bible Dictionary*, 2nd ed., Tyndale Publishing Co., 1962, pp. 692, 1215, 421)

A Tragic Cycle
Based on Judges 2:11-19

DEFINING THE ISSUE

Gene DuPont lay staring at the ceiling. How did this happen? He looked over at his wife Gabrielle, who lay with her back turned to him. He knew by her uneven breathing she was not asleep and was probably crying silently.

They were sure it was the Lord who had blessed them as they moved up the ranks on their jobs. But with the promotions came situations they had not counted on. Like having to attend all those social functions—barbeques and cocktail parties. They didn't drink at these events—not at first—and they were also brave enough to leave early when they had a commitment at church—at first. They used to refuse invitations to work-related social gatherings on Sundays. They took all the ribbing about their lifestyle in good humor.

Then something happened. Gene became the "good ole' boy," and Gabby became the "chic" one to have at parties. But Gene and Gabrielle didn't realize just how closely their co-workers were watching them. Or maybe they did, and after a while, they forgot. Until tonight. Tonight, they found themselves drinking and partying and flirting right along with the best of them. They figured to themselves, "God put us here in these positions. He knows we can handle it. I guess this is what you call 'Christian liberty.' Hey, it ain't that serious."

Then Gabrielle walked into the plush den of Mr. Drew, her boss, to freshen her drink. Mr. Drew was there alone. He approached her and tried to make a play for her. She called for Gene, who came in and threatened to hit him.

"Oh, come on, you two hypocrites," Mr. Drew had said. "You're no different than the rest of us. You're out teaching us old dogs some new tricks. You know, you almost had me convinced about this Christianity bit. I almost thought there was some hope." That scene played over and over in Gene's mind.

Gabrielle turned over and faced Gene. "We need to pray for help, honey. We can't keep going this way."

"I know," Gene replied, "and we don't want this to become a habit—doing our thing, and then having to go to the Lord all shame-faced for deliverance and forgiveness. We won't walk away from our jobs, but they'll know God forgives and Christians do get their acts together—and keep their acts together."

AIM

By the end of the lesson, students will be able to recite Israel's tragic behavior pattern, will understand the causes of their ups and downs, and will determine to be consistent in their personal Christian behavior and to influence such behavior in their homes.

SCRIPTURE TEXT

> JUDGES 2:11 And the children of Israel did evil in the sight of the Lord, and served Baalim:
>
> 12 And they forsook the Lord God of their fathers, which brought them out of the land of Egypt, and

followed other gods, of the gods of the people that were round about them, and bowed themselves unto them, and provoked the Lord to anger.

13 And they forsook the Lord, and served Baal and Ashtaroth.

14 And the anger of the Lord was hot against Israel, and he delivered them into the hands of spoilers that spoiled them, and he sold them into the hands of their enemies round about, so that they could not any longer stand before their enemies.

15 Whithersoever they went out, the hand of the Lord was against them for evil, as the Lord had said, and as the Lord had sworn unto them: and they were greatly distressed.

16 Nevertheless the Lord raised up judges, which delivered them out of the hand of those that spoiled them.

17 And yet they would not hearken unto their judges, but they went a-whoring after other gods, and bowed themselves unto them: they turned quickly out of the way which their fathers walked in, obeying the commandments of the Lord; but they did not so.

18 And when the Lord raised them up judges, then the Lord was with the judge, and delivered them out of the hand of their enemies all the days of the judge: for it repented the Lord because of their groanings by reason of them that oppressed them and vexed them.

19 And it came to pass, when the judge was dead, that they returned, and corrupted themselves more than

their fathers, in following other gods to serve them, and to bow down unto them; they ceased not from their own doings, nor from their stubborn way.

BIBLE BACKGROUND

The Book of Judges is a history of the 13 judges who ruled over Israel for the period of time between when Joshua died and the installation of Saul to be king. The estimated duration is between 200 and 400 years. The term "judge" did not have the same meaning we apply to it today. It did not mean sitting and hearing cases. The Hebrew term is *shophetim*, which means a magistrate or ruler (*Strong's Exhaustive Concordance*).

The Book of Ruth was actually a part of the Book of Judges until around 450 A.D., when it was separated and placed after Song of Solomon in the Hebrew Scriptures. Although there is some uncertainty about the authorship of Judges, it is generally attributed to the Prophet Samuel. The book records God's constant deliverance of Israel by the judges, despite repeated failure to adhere to the faith of their fathers and remain loyal to the one true God.

POINTS TO PONDER

1. *Why did God become angry with Israel? (Judges 2:11-13)*
2. *What were the consequences of their idolatry? (vv. 14-15)*
3. *How did God in His mercy deliver the Israelites? (v. 16)*
4. *What was the people's response to the judges? (v. 17)*
5. *Why did God continue to rescue His people? (v. 18)*

LESSON AT-A-GLANCE

1. *Rebellion (Judges 2:11-13)*

2. *Retribution (vv. 14-15)*
3. *Rescue (vv. 16-18)*
4. *Regression (v. 19)*

EXPLORING THE MEANING

1. Rebellion (Judges 2:11-13)

At times, it's easy to miss the full meaning of things in the Scriptures. That's why it's so necessary to read and re-read the Word of God.

Verse 11 makes two statements which require some meditation. First, it states that the children of Israel did evil "in the sight of the Lord." They did evil knowing that God was watching—as the young people say, "in His face," and as the Hebrew word *ayin* (for eye), implies. Second, it states that they served Baalim. Baalim is plural for Baal, the "god of choice" in Canaan at the time. They served not one, but many gods.

They left the "God of their fathers" (v. 12).

Judges 2:10 states that this was a generation which did not know God, neither were they aware of the works God had done for their forefathers. The parents obviously did not share with them the rich history of their people and the wonderful things God had done in bringing them into the Promised Land. This generation was born in the Promised Land and had no conception of the struggle to get there.

The statements made in verse 10 also imply that consistent worship was sorely lacking among the Israelites. Had worship been consistent and included the celebration of the Passover, at some point the leadership would have reminded the people of what God had done during the Exodus, the wilderness experience, and the entrance into the Promised Land.

57

Yet they were not totally ignorant. Verses 12 and 13 state that they "forsook" the Lord. They left Him and served Baal and Ashtaroth. Baal was the principal male god of Canaan. Baal was the "storm god," and each province had their own version of him. Ashtaroth is a plural form of Ashtoreth, the female goddess of the land. She represented the passive side of nature. Each of these deities was present in other societies under other names. For example, Ashtoreth to the Assyrians was Ishtar, and to the Greeks, Astarte. Each Baal had a wife. The qualities attributed to these idols reflect certain aspects of the cultures which worshiped them. Women in these cultures were passive to the point of being used as temple prostitutes and virgins saved for sacrifices. Men were valued for their strength and fierceness. Baal and Ashtoreth are two of the gods the Israelites CHOSE to serve.

2. Retribution (vv. 14-15)

The Lord was angry. The word used in verse 14 is "hot," which means glowing and growing in intensity. God's anger had been building. They had a written record of His warnings and of the consequences of their actions (see Deuteronomy 28). God kept His word and allowed them to be plundered; they could not defeat their enemies in battle. He "sold" them into the hands of their enemies as a Canaanite would give a daughter into slavery to pay a debt. Wherever they went, God no longer fought for them; therefore, they were not victorious over their enemies.

Christians have been so tuned to the eternal loving kindness of the Lord, and have so often talked of His mercy and grace, that often we forget that God can become angry.

The Israelites are now described as "distressed" (v. 15) (yatsar), pressed up against a wall, pressed like a ripe olive. Those they have tried to imitate and whose gods they have adopted have become their slave masters. Yet the Israelites refused to change the lifestyle which caused them to be in bondage.

3. Rescue (vv. 16-18)
In spite of Israel's sins, God brought judges on the scene to deliver them from their enemies. The judges had the responsibility of not only delivering the people, usually through war, but of being their spiritual leaders—a task some were reluctant to accept. Barak, for example, would not fight unless Deborah went. And Samson was a womanizer who wanted to be buddies with the Philistines.

Even while their judge was alive and working, the Israelites still worshiped other gods. Of their own choice, they went against the counsel of the judges and did not obey the commandments of the Lord. They refused to listen. Unfortunately, some of the judges were not exactly beacons of light either, which made the situation even more difficult. Remember Samson? And Gideon caused Israel to go "a-whoring" (v. 17) after the ephod he created (8:27).

This tragic pattern of living left an entire generation of God's people in a sad state of affairs. They were in a vicious spiritual cycle of rebellion, retribution, rescue, and then….

4. Regression (v. 19)
Notice, verse 18 does not say "the Lord was with the people." It states that God was "with the judge" for the purpose of delivering the Israelites from the hands of their enemies. God had not forgotten that the entire blame for their constant backsliding did not fully rest with them. It also rested with their parents who had not followed after the Lord wholeheartedly and had not taught and guided their children in the ways of the Lord. So the Lord pitied their groanings because of the oppression they were under, and He delivered them through the judges.

Is there a tendency among some Christians to attempt to "play games" with God like the Israelites did? The Israelites flaunted their unfaithfulness in the face of God. Yet when they got into trouble, it was not Baal or Ashtaroth they cried out to. It was the God of their fathers. Still, they would leave the Lord again and again. They wanted the best of both worlds, as many people do today. They wanted to fulfill selfish desires and to have God available as a safety net. To such people, the New Testament message is clear: "Be not deceived; God is not mocked: for whatsoever a man soweth, that shall he also reap. For he that soweth to his flesh shall of the flesh reap corruption; but he that soweth to the Spirit shall of the Spirit reap life everlasting" (Galatians 6:7-8).

In addition to the tragic pattern of living we are prone to practice when we do not follow God fully, there are three other points of value to be considered:

A. Failure to please God is our responsibility. The fact that they were called "the children of Israel" (Judges 2:11), and that "they forsook the Lord" (v. 12) means they were not totally ignorant of the Lord and understood to some degree that they belonged to Him. Therefore, in spite of the void left in their upbringing by their parents, they bore some responsibility for their situation. We often blame others for our failure to live the life that pleases God, but the real responsibility is ours.

B. The choice to please God is our decision. It is stated that "they bowed themselves" (v. 12), meaning they were not coerced. It was a voluntary action. It was their choice. Often, a Christian's argument in prayer goes something like this, "Lord, if You had…then I wouldn't have…." That is placing the blame for our sins on God. "Let no man say when he is tempted, I am tempted of God" (James 1:13). God is sovereign; He is in complete control. He can do what He wants, when He wants, where He wants, to whom He wants. Yet, He is gracious enough to make promises to us through His Holy Word about what He will and will not do. When we disagree with Him and move in another direction, it is called rebellion. God is not against us, He is for us. If we choose not to obey Him, He will not coerce us; but if we choose to obey Him, He will help us.

C. If we choose not to obey the Lord, negative consequences will follow. Rebellion is a waste of time, energy, and resources that can be put to better use by being a blessing to others. When we rebel in the face of God, we suffer the consequences in the face of the world. The world then becomes a bit more hardened to spiritual things, and to the love of God. Our witness is rendered less effective or ineffective. We lose credibility in the eyes of the very people we are trying to influence.

For African Americans to continue reaching back 300 years to justify negative and destructive behavior not only displeases God, it disturbs other African Americans as well.

This is not to say that we have not been mistreated and still bear in our personalities the scars of slavery and racism. But isn't it time for us to turn from our wicked ways, to seek God in humble prayer, so that He can forgive our sin and heal us individually and collectively? Isn't it time for that?

DISCERNING MY DUTY

1. *After all God had done for them, Israel still worshiped idol gods. Why do you think this was so?*

2. *When a judge died, the people immediately returned to idolatry. What are some possible reasons for this?*
3. *Why did the Israelites not listen to the very people who were sent to deliver them?*
4. *The Lord sends African American leaders such as Booker T. Washington, Mary Bethune, and Martin Luther King, Jr. To what extent have Americans heeded their messages and followed their instructions?*

DECIDING MY RESPONSE

To think about—It has been stated that Americans are endangering themselves by paralleling the tragic pattern of the Israelites: turning away from the true God, practicing immoral behavior, getting into trouble, crying out to God, being delivered, and starting the pattern all over again. The Moseses, Joshuas, and judges of this century have continually called us to remember our God, to follow His ways, and hold on to our heritage. The consequences of refusing to listen to them have included: increased unwed motherhood, absentee fatherhood, gang wars, alcohol and drug abuse, financial and emotional distress. Do you agree with this assessment? Explain.

1. What are some of the parallels between the history of the Israelites and American history?
2. As a people, have African Americans been more faithful to God than the Israelites?
3. Have American parents and teachers been more diligent in teaching their children about God than the Israelite parents?
4. Are Americans of this generation less inclined or more inclined to put other things, people, and activities before the worship and service of God?

To do—New laws are enacted every day in an attempt to keep society under control. The highest level of morality, however, cannot be legislated. It must be taught and lived. God's ways are unbelievably simple: it starts at home. Home and church can once again become the centers of living for the family. Here are some suggestions to encourage family unity:

1. Turn off the television, radio, VCR, and CD player at least one evening this week.
2. Eat dinner together.
3. Talk about what the Lord has meant/means in your life, have family prayer, and attend church together.

If this is a new experiment, do not expect it to go perfectly, but try it lovingly and persistently for a month. Discuss the experience with the class.

WHAT I WILL DO

_____
_____
_____
_____
_____

LIGHT ON THE HEAVY

JUDGES. Judges were those raised up by God to teach the Israelites God's will and deliver the Israelites from the oppression of their enemies. While the position was for life, it was not hereditary and could not be passed to the children of the judge. Some of the more famous judges included Deborah, Gideon, and Samson, but there were others—Tola, Jair, Ibzan, Elon, and Abdon—of whom we know nothing other than the fact that they served as judges.

The entire rule of the judges is divided into four periods. Outside of the Book of Judges, Eli, a priest, is regarded as also having held the office of judge, as well as Samuel the prophet. After the judges, Saul served as their first king. (*Guideposts Bible Dictionary*, 1984, p. 363)

Seizing An Opportunity
Based on 1 Samuel 9:15-17; 10:1, 20-24

DEFINING THE ISSUE

Fear gripped Lillie's heart as she read the Sunday church service program. She had been chosen to open the service in prayer. She knew that something like this would happen one day because Pastor Turner believed, "Since we're all a part of the body, we should all be willing to do whatever's necessary to help the body function properly."

Lillie didn't mind helping out, but she always felt a little inadequate. There were plenty of people in the congregation who she felt could do a much better job. The more Lillie thought about it, the more she wanted to find someplace to hide. In her imagination, she saw herself standing in front of all those people and no words coming out.

Lillie sat in her seat and silently prayed. When the time came, she walked to the front of the church and silently said, "Lord, it's all up to You now." Then she opened her mouth and lifted up a beautiful prayer of praise and thanksgiving.

Assuming positions of leadership exposes feelings of inadequacy in many people. God always selects ordinary people to accomplish His purposes. This lesson tells the story of Saul and his feeling of inadequacy when he suddenly became king of Israel.

AIM

By the end of the lesson, students will able to: recall the events that led to the selection of Saul as Israel's first king; express how God controls people and events to accomplish His purposes; understand how God prepares people for the tasks He assigns them; find their place in God's plan and go to work.

SCRIPTURE TEXT

> 1 SAMUEL 9:15 Now the Lord had told Samuel in his ear a day before Saul came, saying,
>
> 16 Tomorrow about this time I will send thee a man out of the land of Benjamin, and thou shalt anoint him to be captain over my people Israel, that he may save my people out of the hand of the Philistines: for I have looked upon my people, because their cry is come unto me.
>
> 17 And when Samuel saw Saul, the Lord said unto him, Behold the man whom I spake to thee of! this same shall reign over my people.
>
> 10:1 Then Samuel took a vial of his oil, and poured it upon his head, and kissed him, and said, Is it not because the Lord hath anointed thee to be captain over his inheritance?
>
> 20 And when Samuel had caused all the tribes of Israel to come near, the tribe of Benjamin was taken.
>
> 21 When he had caused the tribe of Benjamin to come near by their families, the family of Matri was taken, and Saul the son of Kish was taken: and when they sought him, he could not be found.

22 Therefore they inquired of the Lord further, if the man should yet come thither. And the Lord answered, Behold, he hath hid himself among the stuff.

23 And they ran and fetched him thence: and when he stood among the people, he was higher than any of the people from his shoulders and upward.

24 And Samuel said to all the people, See ye him whom the Lord hath chosen, that there is none like him among all the people? And all the people shouted, and said, God save the king.

BIBLE BACKGROUND

Some people believe that life is just a series of random happenings. Others believe in a non-personal force called fate which pre-determines events. George MacDonald, a 19th century writer stated, "The next hour, the next moment, is as much beyond our grasp and as much in God's care, as that a hundred years away."

Have you ever wondered why some of the events that take place in your life happen the way they do? Is it possible that some of these things may be acts of divine providence? The dictionary defines providence as "making arrangements for future events or needs beforehand." So divine providence is probably best defined as God directing people and events to prepare beforehand for future needs. The story of the meeting between Saul and the Prophet Samuel beautifully illustrates God's control over the events of life. Saul is the man who went out looking for some lost donkeys and found a kingdom. Read the story in 1 Samuel 9:1-14.

POINTS TO PONDER

1. *The Old Testament word for "seer" means one who sees ahead. What were seers later called in Israel? (1 Samuel 9:9)*

2. *Although the people demanded a king, who really chose Saul to be ruler over Israel? (v. 15)*

3. *God and Samuel had a close personal relationship. What are the words used to illustrate this relationship? (v. 15)*

4. *In the United States, leaders are installed into office by placing their hands on the Bible and swearing an oath. How were the leaders of ancient Israel installed? (10:1)*

5. *Where was Saul during his public presentation as the divinely chosen king? (v. 22)*

6. *How did the people respond when Saul was announced as God's choice to rule Israel? (v. 24)*

LESSON AT-A-GLANCE

1. *God chooses Saul (1 Samuel 9:15-17)*
2. *Samuel privately anoints Saul (10:1)*
3. *Samuel publicly anoints Saul (vv. 20-24)*

EXPLORING THE MEANING

1. God chooses Saul (1 Samuel 9:15-17)

God had revealed to Samuel the day before meeting Saul that a man from the tribe of Benjamin would come to see him. He was to anoint this man leader over Israel. Verse 15 says that God told this to Samuel in his ear, which indicates the close relationship between God and Samuel. It is significant that Saul is called a captain or leader rather than king (v. 16). This is because the throne was promised to the line of Judah (Genesis 49:10), and Saul was from the line of Benjamin. When Samuel saw Saul coming, the Lord again spoke to him, saying, "This is the man I spoke to you about; he will govern my people" (1 Samuel 9:17, NIV).

Psalm 37:23 says, "The steps of a good man are ordered by the Lord." This is true even in times that appear to be failures. Notice how God uses the sequence of events to bring about His will: 1) the nation wanted a king (1 Samuel 8:4-5); 2) the donkeys were lost (9:3); 3) Saul's search for them ended in failure (v. 4); 4) his search ended near the city where Samuel lived (v. 6); 5) Saul just happened to "run into" Samuel and ask him for directions (v. 18). Even in the darkest times of life, isn't it a blessing to know that God is in control and working things out for our good and His divine purposes? (Romans 8:28)

2. Samuel privately anoints Saul (10:1)

It's easy to imagine the difficulty Saul had trying to figure out what was going on. He had come looking for lost donkeys, but before he could even ask the question, Samuel told him the animals had been found. Then Samuel informed Saul that the most desirable thing in all Israel, being a king, belonged to him and his family.

Saul certainly did not see himself as deserving such an honor. He responded to Samuel's lavish treatment by stating that he was from the humblest family in the smallest tribe of Israel. At the sacrificial feast Saul was seated in the place of honor and given the choice portion of meat which had been set aside for him in advance (9:18-24).

The next day Samuel privately anointed Saul ruler over Israel (10:1). Anointing was the Old Testament ritual of consecration. It involved pouring or rubbing oil on the person, an indication that the anointed one was now infused with the power of God and set apart for service to the Lord.

3. Samuel publicly anoints Saul (vv. 20-24)

Imagine that one day you're going about your life as usual, and the next day, without any prior warning, you're suddenly chosen to be the President of the United States. This is similar to what happened to Saul. He was a farmer with no desire or training to rule people, but God had chosen him in spite of his shortcomings.

Shortly after Samuel's private anointing, Saul was publicly presented to the nation at Mizpah. So that the people would know the choice was God's, they cast lots using the Urim and Thummin. By asking questions, and then tossing the lots like dice, the people were assured of God's answer. What might appear to be pure chance was actually controlled by God.

Using this process, the selection is narrowed down to one tribe, one family, and finally one man. Saul was the chosen one, but when he was named he was absent. Poor Saul, overcome by the fear of this tremendous undesired responsibility, had hidden himself among the people's luggage. After the people searched in vain for the reluctant Saul, God revealed where he was hiding. They brought Saul out and stood him before the people. He was taller than everyone else. Samuel proclaimed that Saul was the one the Lord had chosen and that there was no one else in all Israel like him. The people responded by shouting, "Long live the king!"

It has been said that the strong are not always vigorous, the wise are not always ready, the brave are not always courageous, and the joyous are not always happy. Sometimes it is normal to feel overwhelmed by responsibilities, but a truth about God is that *He doesn't always call the equipped, but He always equips the called.* Verse 9 says that as Saul turned to leave Samuel, God gave him a new heart. The Spirit of God endowed him with all the qualities necessary to rule.

If we cooperate with Him, the Lord who calls us will also equip us for our assigned task. Does our cooperation mean getting more education, reading books, listening to tapes, taking specialized classes, spending more time in prayer and Bible study? Whatever it takes, it's worth it to be effective in our work for the Lord.

DISCERNING MY DUTY

1. *How would you describe the difference between fate and divine providence?*

2. *In the United States, leaders are chosen by popular vote. Do you believe divine providence plays a role in this process? Why?*

3. *"Spiritual anointing is bestowed on believers by God through the Holy Spirit." What does that mean?*

4. *Why do you think God would choose a person for a position of responsibility when that person feels unable to do the job?*

DECIDING MY RESPONSE

To think about—1. Do you think the Civil War of the last century and the Civil Rights Movement of the '60s were acts of divine providence or simply happenstance? Why?

2. In what ways do you think our society would be different if every Christian accepted his divinely appointed responsibilities?

3. In what ways would your home, neighborhood, or workplace be different if you accepted your divinely appointed responsibility?

To do—God saved all of us for a purpose. This week, ask the Lord to reveal what He wants you to do to serve Him by serving people.

Ask Him for the power to carry out your mission and begin your assignment this week.

WHAT I WILL DO

_____
_____
_____
_____
_____

LIGHT ON THE HEAVY

THE UNITED MONARCHY. Israel underwent a drastic change when theocracy (rule by God) gave way to monarchy (rule by a king). This period of history is usually divided into two parts, the United Kingdom (ca. 1043-930 B.C.) and the Divided Kingdoms (ca. 930-586 B.C.). Particularly in the first period, the governmental structure grew more complex.

Israel became a monarchy when Saul was enthroned. The Israelites had been oppressed by the Philistines for many years and wanted to have "a king to judge us like all the nations" (1 Samuel 8:5). They wanted a permanent military leader who would keep them free of other nations' rule. The words "a king to judge" probably emphasize the military role that the judges played in preceding centuries, rather than the judicial role of settling disputes among the people.

CHOOSING A KING. The king was chosen by God (1 Samuel 9:15-16), as well as by the people (1 Samuel 11:15). But the people's demand for a king was seen as rejection of God's military leadership; they wanted deliverance from their enemies without obedience to God. Had their attitude toward God been different,

God would have provided a king for His people in due course. This event had been planned for centuries before (see Deuteronomy 17:14-20). God agreed to their request but predicted judgment against them. Ultimately, the king would oppress the people through heavy taxation and by drafting people to work for him and serve in his army (see 1 Samuel 8:9-18).

Government under King Saul continued to be quite simple, for he did not make any known changes from the previous ways. We know of no administrative or bureaucratic developments during his reign. His only administrators seemed to have been members of his family. His son Jonathan and his cousin Abner served with him in the army and led the militia (1 Samuel 13:1-2, 16; 14:50-51). We also find that Saul established a permanent army in keeping with the desire of the people (1 Samuel 14:52). (J. I. Packer, et al. *The Bible Almanac*, Nashville: Thomas Nelson Publishers, 1980, p. 322)

A House Divided
Based on 1 Kings 12:13-17, 20-29

DEFINING THE ISSUE

The independent Black church was born in protest to racism and discrimination. Richard Allen and a small group of Black persons attended St. George Methodist Episcopal Church in Philadelphia. However, when more Blacks began to attend, the White church members changed their seating from where they usually sat and placed them around the wall. Blacks were segregated in and alienated from the same church to which they made significant financial and constructional contributions.

One Sunday morning when the Blacks were kneeling for prayer during worship, having been physically attacked for not sitting in their own section by impatient Whites who could not wait until the prayer was ended, Richard Allen and the Blacks who were joined with him left the church, eventually organizing the African Methodist Episcopal Church (1791). This was the first of all Black denominations in America.

Perhaps if those Whites who mistreated the Black members at St. George M.E. Church would have realized what their inhumane attitudes and precipitant actions would lead to, they would not have acted so foolishly. Yet, their lack of brotherhood was the straw which ultimately broke the camel's back of unity. The racial divisions within the Church in America, which in a very real sense were already instituted and propagated by Whites against Blacks, became critical. The Church in America has yet to recover from such racial disharmony.

This focuses our study. The foolishness of Rehoboam led to the division of the kingdom of Israel—a division in the nation which never healed.

AIM

By the end of the session, students should realize that thoughtless and rash attitudes can lead to disastrous consequences regarding unity, and will make every effort to sustain unity in their families, churches, and communities.

SCRIPTURE TEXT

> 1 KINGS 12:13 And the king answered the people roughly, and forsook the old men's counsel that they gave him;
>
> 14 And spake to them after the counsel of the young men, saying, My father made your yoke heavy, and I will add to your yoke: my father also chastised you with whips, but I will chastise you with scorpions.
>
> 15 Wherefore the king hearkened not unto the people; for the cause was from the Lord, that he might perform his saying, which the Lord spake by Ahijah the Shilonite unto Jeroboam the son of Nebat.
>
> 16 So when all Israel saw that the king hearkened not unto them, the people answered the king, saying, What portion have we in David? neither have we inheritance

in the son of Jesse: to your tents, O Israel: now see to thine own house, David. So Israel departed unto their tents.

17 But as for the children of Israel which dwelt in the cities of Judah, Rehoboam reigned over them.

20 And it came to pass, when all Israel heard that Jeroboam was come again, that they sent and called him unto the congregation, and made him king over all Israel: there was none that followed the house of David, but the tribe of Judah only.

26 And Jeroboam said in his heart, Now shall the kingdom return to the house of David:

27 If this people go up to do sacrifice in the house of the Lord at Jerusalem, then shall the heart of this people turn again unto their lord, even unto Rehoboam king of Judah, and they shall kill me, and go again to Rehoboam king of Judah.

28 Whereupon the king took counsel, and made two calves of gold, and said unto them, It is too much for you to go up to Jerusalem: behold thy gods, O Israel, which brought thee up out of the land of Egypt.

29 And he set the one in Bethel, and the other put he in Dan.

BIBLE BACKGROUND

Solomon loved many foreign women, 700 of whom became his wives and 300 his concubines. Undoubtedly, he formed many of these relationships for political expediency. As Solomon became older, his women drew his heart away from following the Lord.

The Lord became angry with Solomon because of his sin and pronounced judgment upon him after warning him twice. The kingdom would be taken from Solomon and given to one of his subordinates. Only for the sake of David would the Lord stay the chastisement until Solomon had died. Solomon's son would reap the consequences.

Following the death of Solomon (1 Kings 11:41-43), everything fell apart. Verses 1-24 of 1 Kings 12 deals with the revolt and secession of the northern tribes, and verses 25-33 cover the evil plans of Jeroboam.

POINTS TO PONDER

1. *How did Rehoboam answer the people, and whose counsel did he reject? (1 Kings 12:13)*
2. *How was the sovereign God working in this experience? (v. 15)*
3. *How did the people respond to the bullheadedness of Rehoboam? (v. 16)*
4. *Who did the seceding tribes of Israel choose as their king? (v. 20)*
5. *Why did Jeroboam institute centers of worship in the northern kingdom? (v. 27)*
6. *What objects of worship did Jeroboam make, and where did he place them in his kingdom? (vv. 28-29)*

LESSON AT-A-GLANCE

1. *The problem causing the division (1 Kings 12:13-15)*
2. *The pronounced nature of the division (vv. 16-17, 20)*
3. *The perpetuation of the division (vv. 12:26-29)*

EXPLORING THE MEANING

1. The problem causing the division (1 Kings 12:13-15)
Rehoboam, Solomon's son, succeeded his father on the throne of Israel and proceeded to Shechem for his coronation. In the meantime, a delegation of Israelites (perhaps the senior people), representing a majority of the people included in the northern tribes, sent for Jeroboam to come from exile in Egypt to be their spokesman (12:1-3).

The people requested of Rehoboam one thing: "lighten our load." They would give their support only if the relief was forthcoming. Rehoboam considered the matter for three days (12:1-5).

What should be done? Rehoboam asked the elders who had served Solomon. The elders counseled him to lighten the people's load. Their wisdom showed that the people would serve Rehoboam for life. Rehoboam rejected the elders' advice (vv. 6-8a).

What should be done? Rehoboam asked the young men who were his peers and now had received a piece of the kingdom action. The young men counseled him to make the load of the people heavier. There was no wisdom in this counsel (vv. 8b-12).

As the story goes, Rehoboam followed the advice of his peers. When the people assembled on the third day to hear his response, Rehoboam spoke to the people harshly, unnecessarily antagonizing them. In an emotionally charged assembly, with their feelings open and their expectations raised, Rehoboam crushed the appeal and hopes of the people. He told them he would not only continue the policies of his father, he would intensify them. Resolutely, Rehoboam would make the people's burden heavier (vv. 13-15).

This turn of events was from the Lord. He would use the recalcitrance of Rehoboam to fulfill the prophecy of Ahijah concerning the division of the kingdom (v. 15; 1 Kings 11:29 ff.).

A number of historical factors contributed to the division of the kingdom. However, it was the stubborn attitude of Rehoboam which exacerbated the situation.

2. The pronounced nature of the division (12:16-17, 20)
Immediately the bullheadedness of Rehoboam affected the people of Israel. It was clear that Rehoboam would not listen to the people, not even the elders (vv. 8, 13, 15, 16). His obstinacy served only to solidify his opposition. Since Rehoboam did what he had to do, they did what they had to do! In essence, the people said to Rehoboam, "Since we have no meaningful participation in your kingdom, we will take care of our own business! And you take care of yours!" (cf. 2 Samuel 20:1) So the people went home to organize a separate kingdom. Only Judah remained under Rehoboam's leadership (vv. 16-17).

Rehoboam sent his taskmaster Adoram to deal with the people's revolt. "All Israel stoned him to death!" (v. 18) Rehoboam barely managed to save his own neck. The people of Israel crowned Jeroboam the leader of their newly organized nation (v. 20).

From this point forward there existed two separated kingdoms: Israel in the north with nine or ten tribes, and Judah in the south, with two or three tribes (Judah, Benjamin, and Simeon; cf. *Zondervan Pictorial Bible Encyclopedia*, "Israel, History of"; vol. 3, p. 343). The rift was permanent: two kings, two capitals, two administrations, two systems of priesthood, two armies, etc.

3. The perpetuation of the division (12:26-29)
Rehoboam sought to regain control of the entire kingdom through military force, but he was dissuaded by the Prophet Shemaiah.

They must not fight against their brothers, but let God's will be done. (This would have been good advice for the Methodists, who made every effort, including threats of disowning Blacks and putting them out of the Conference, to prevent Richard Allen and his group from starting an independent church.)

Now Jeroboam king of Israel becomes a problem. Fearing that the northern kingdom, desiring to worship God at the temple in Jerusalem, would eventually revert to the leadership of Rehoboam, he institutes some ungodly changes (vv. 26-28).

Jeroboam made two golden calves, which he referred to as the gods who brought Israel out of Egypt. One he placed in the southern part of his territory in the city of Bethel (just 12 miles from Jerusalem), and the other in the city of Dan in the north. The Lord condemned this idolatry (v. 30; 14:9, 10). Moreover, in violation of the Mosaic code, Jeroboam constructed high places throughout the land and appointed non-Levitical priests to offer sacrifices on the altar. He instituted a festival on a day of his own choosing (not God's day). As self-appointed chief priest, he did his own officiating at the altar at Bethel (vv. 28-33).

If Jeroboam had been faithful to the Lord, the Lord would have been with him to bless him (11:37-39). As it stands, his name in the Sacred Writ has come down to us in infamy. It was Jeroboam's entrenched sin which sealed the division of the kingdom.

DISCERNING MY DUTY

1. *Why is division among the people of God so reprehensible?*
2. *How is it possible for God to use the sinful mistakes of people to accomplish His will?*
3. *What are some negative attitudes that can prove defeating for those who lead God's people?*

4. *How can mutual participation in decision-making and a caring attitude bring healing to the body of Christ?*
5. *Why are fear of man, loss of power, and loss of reputation bad motives from which to operate?*
6. *What should the White Church in America do to foster harmony with the Black Church? What should the Black Church do?*

DECIDING MY RESPONSE

Pair off with someone who will be frank in discussing negative attitudes that you have. Take at least one full hour during the week to confidentially and lovingly discuss one another's attitudes. Also, focus on one potential problem affecting the unity of the Church and suggest some ways to solve that problem.

WHAT I WILL DO

_____
_____
_____

LIGHT ON THE HEAVY

SCORPION—Verse 14. A spider-like insect with claws that give it a lobster look. The tail has poison in it which stings. It is therefore feared. The scorpion-like punishment which Rehoboam promised to inflict on the Israelites was probably not to be taken literally. He probably meant that the pain would be so severe that it would appear to be that of scorpions.

TENTS—Verse 16. Tents were temporary shelters, often made of goats' hair cloth stretched over poles and held in place by cords. The word could refer to any dwelling place.

God Uses Obedient People
Based on 2 Kings 5:1-14

DEFINING THE ISSUE

"It won't work." "It's too simple." Try it—what do you have to lose?" How often have we heard these three statements uttered from the lips of both friend and foe?

The focus of this Bible study is a man who thought the instructions for his healing were too simple. He was sure "it wouldn't work." The one thing he had to lose was leprosy, so he reluctantly obeyed the command of the man of God. His remarkable healing was made possible because a number of people were obedient to the Lord.

AIM

By the end of the study, participants will be able to describe how several people obeyed the Lord, will be convinced that obedience to God brings satisfaction to both themselves and to God, and will make a commitment to faithfully obey the known will of God.

SCRIPTURE TEXT

> 2 KINGS 5:1 Now Naaman, captain of the host of the king of Syria, was a great man with his master, and honourable, because by him the Lord had given deliverance

unto Syria: he was also a mighty man in valour, but he was a leper.

2 And the Syrians had gone out by companies, and had brought away captive out of the land of Israel a little maid; and she waited on Naaman's wife.

3 And she said unto her mistress, Would God my lord were with the prophet that is in Samaria! For he would recover him of his leprosy.

4 And one went in, and told his lord, saying, Thus and thus said the maid that is of the land of Israel.

5 And the king of Syria said, Go to, go, and I will send a letter unto the king of Israel. And he departed, and took with him ten talents of silver, and six thousand pieces of gold, and ten changes of raiment.

9 So Naaman came with his horses and with his chariot, and stood at the door of the house of Elisha.

10 And Elisha sent a messenger unto him, saying, Go and wash in Jordan seven times, and thy flesh shall come again to thee, and thou shalt be clean.

11 But Naaman was wroth, and went away, and said, Behold, I thought, He will surely come to me, and stand, and call on the name of the Lord his God, and strike his hand over the place, and recover the leper.

12 Are not Abana and Pharpar, rivers of Damascus, better than all the waters of Israel? may I not wash in them, and be clean? So he turned and went away in a rage.

13 And his servants came near, and spake unto him, and said, My father, if the prophet had bid thee do

some great thing, wouldest thou not have done it? how much rather then, when he saith to thee, Wash, and be clean?

14 Then went he down, and dipped himself seven times in Jordan, according to the saying of the man of God: and his flesh came again like unto the flesh of a little child, and he was clean.

BIBLE BACKGROUND

The events described in this text take place during the time Elisha the prophet lived. The northern kingdom of Israel is ruled by Joram. Ben-hadad II is the king of Syria. A fragile truce exists between Israel and Syria.

Naaman was commander-in-chief of the armies of Ben-hadad II. This high-ranking soldier was known for his bravery in war, including wars with Israel. He was trusted and admired by his king, and they celebrated many victories.

It is not known whether Naaman contracted leprosy through heredity, or through some unknown contact, but the law required Israelites to wear a mourning costume, rumple their hair, live in isolation, and cry "unclean" whenever people were near (see Leviticus 13, especially 13:45, 46).

Ten talents of silver (about $20,000), 6,000 pieces of gold (perhaps $60,000), and ten complete suits for festive occasions were to be his gift of gratitude for the healing he expected to receive from the prophet of God.

POINTS TO PONDER

1. *What position did Naaman hold, and why was he so honored by the King of Syria? (2 Kings 5:1)*

2. What type of sickness did Naaman have? (v. 1)
3. What did the little slave girl tell Naaman's wife? (v. 3)
4. How did the King of Syria respond to Naaman? (v. 5)
5. What did Naaman take with him? (v. 5)
6. After having arrived at Elisha's home, what was Naaman told, and by whom? (v. 10)
7. How did Naaman respond to Elisha's instructions? (vv. 1, 12)
8. Who convinced Naaman to do as the prophet had instructed? (v. 13)
9. What happened when Naaman dipped himself seven times in the Jordan River, according to the instructions of the Prophet Elisha? (v. 14)

LESSON AT-A-GLANCE

1. *God used a female slave (2 Kings 5:1-5, 9)*
2. *God used an obedient prophet (vv. 10-12)*
3. *God used a male servant (v. 13)*
4. *God healed an obedient man (v. 14)*

EXPLORING THE MEANING
1. God used a female slave (2 Kings 5:1-5, 9)

During one of the wars between Syria and Israel, a Hebrew girl was captured. To be enslaved is a sad and tragic event. But this account illustrates how God used a slave girl to turn an evil circumstance into a blessing for her captor.

Scripture does not say, but it can be assumed that the slave girl had observed the dreaded disease of her master. "He was a leper" (KJV). The New Bible Commentary, Revised says the word leprosy "rarely if ever refers to the disease referred to as 'leprosy' today." The exact nature of the disease which afflicted Naaman is not known. But it seems safe to assume that "he suffered from a dreaded skin disease" (TEV). Whatever the disease, it was probably painful, and some commentators suggest it was fatal.

The comment of a slave girl to her mistress set in motion a chain of events which changed the life of her master: "If only my master would see the prophet who is in Samaria! He would cure him of [literally, take away] his leprosy" (v. 3, NIV).

Perhaps her mistress told her husband, Naaman. Naaman followed the necessary protocol; he contacted "his master," King Ben-hadad, who made the necessary arrangements with Joram, king of Israel.

Naaman's wealth is readily perceived from the gifts he took with him. One commentator suggests that "in some sense, Naaman intended to buy his health" (Moore).

2. God used an obedient prophet (2 Kings 5:10-12)

Some Bible scholars suggest that perhaps Joram did not know where Elisha was. Earl notes that it was unlikely that Joram did not know Elisha's whereabouts, since Elisha had recently miraculously restored a dead boy to life (4:32-37). Earl continues: "The miracle did happen at some distance, but Elisha was living in Samaria (v. 3), the capital city, and news of this amazing incident would certainly have spread widely. Probably the truth is that just as Ahab hated Elijah, so his son Joram hated Elijah's successor, Elisha. Most of the kings of the northern kingdom of Israel during this period were wicked idolaters, and they hated the prophets of the Lord."

Whatever the reason, Scripture seems to indicate that Joram had not contacted Elisha prior to Naaman's visit. So, Naaman arrived unannounced, but probably not unexpected.

Naaman arrived at Elisha's house with all the pomp and splendor of a VIP (very important person). He came "with all the horses and chariots" (5:9). Rawlinson comments: "...when the great general, accompanied by a cavalcade of followers, drew up before it, he had, we may be sure, no intention of dismounting and entering."

Neither did Elisha go out to meet Naaman. He sent Naaman's healing instructions by a messenger. It is true that the actions of Naaman and Elisha were essentially the same, but the reasons for their behavior were different.

Why didn't Elisha go out and personally give Naaman the prescription for his healing? Bahr states: "The reason why Elisha did not come out was not that he was wanting in politeness, or that he was influenced by priestly pride, or that he feared the leprosy, or avoided intercourse with a leper in obedience to the law. Elisha remained in his house to impress upon Naaman that neither power nor wealth could buy healing. Elisha wanted to be sure that Naaman understood that his healing was by the grace and power of Almighty God, at the prayer of the prophet."

Conversely, Naaman's pride almost cost him his blessing. Scripture clearly states that Naaman "was angry" because Elisha did not come out and personally address him. Scripture seems to suggest that Naaman anticipated a "big production." Naaman had planned what God would do and how He would do it!

Regarding Naaman's indignation, Rawlinson writes:

"Naaman had imagined a striking scene, whereof he was to be the central figure, the prophet descending, with perhaps a wand of office, the attendants drawn up on either side, the passers-by standing to gaze upon a solemn invocation of the Deity, a waving to and fro of the wand in the prophet's hand, and a sudden manifest cure, wrought in the open street of the city, before the eyes of men, and at once noised abroad through the capital. Instead of this, he is bidden to go as he came, to ride 20 miles to the Jordan, generally muddy, or at least discolored, and there to wash himself, with none to look on but his own attendants, with…no pomp or circumstance, no glory of surroundings. It is not surprising that he was disappointed and vexed."

3. God used a male servant (2 Kings 5:13)
People who are angry do not think clearly. A calm servant helped Naaman to "cool down." He said to Naaman, "My father," (an affectionate address), "why not do what the prophet said." A calmer Naaman is persuaded by his servant to follow the instructions of the prophet.

4. God healed an obedient man (2 Kings 5:14)
Elisha's order to Naaman to "dip in the Jordan" was a simple directive; it was a costless directive. And as soon as Naaman obeyed, he was cured. He went down and dipped himself in the Jordan seven times as the man of God had told him, and his flesh was restored and became clean like that of a young boy.

DISCERNING MY DUTY

1. *Explain how leprosy is like sin.*
2. *Compare Naaman's method of trying to obtain healing with the way many people attempt to obtain salvation.*
3. *Compare the directive Elisha gave Naaman with the directive God gives sinners.*
4. *Compare the result of Naaman's obedience to Elisha's command with the results of man's obedience to God's command.*

DECIDING MY RESPONSE

This week, examine the list that you compiled from the previous study. Select the negative characteristic or habit that you think is most offensive to other people. Read the accompanying verse and pray for deliverance from the characteristic or habit several times daily.

WHAT I WILL DO

_____
_____
_____

LIGHT ON THE HEAVY

LEPROSY. Leprosy was a common but dreaded contagious disease in Biblical times (Luke 4:26-27). It began as spots in the face, ears, forearms, thighs, and buttocks, which later became ulcers (sores) with eventual loss of tissue, then contraction, and finally deformity. Laws of that era stipulated that a leper could not enter a house, which could help to explain why Naaman expected Elisha to come out to him (*Zondervan Pictorial Bible Dictionary*, 1963, p. 218).

A Call for Justice and Righteousness
Based on Amos 4:4-5; 5:18-24

DEFINING THE ISSUE

The Mount Zion Great Day Gospel Choir was the best choir in the church and one of the best in the nation. They were accompanied by skilled musicians and led by outstanding soloists. They gave sold-out concerts and sang at national music workshops and international conventions. They produced albums, cassettes, CDs, and videos. Their feature songs brought crowds to their feet—clapping, shouting, and swaying to the music. But Reverend Amos "sat them down." He told them they couldn't sing anymore anywhere, not even at Mount Zion, until he "gave them the word."

What made Reverend Amos take such drastic action? "There's too much sin in this choir," he said. "And until you all get yourselves right with God, I don't want to hear another note from this choir—not another note!"

Most of the choir and many of the church members at Mount Zion did not agree with Reverend Amos' action. But the prophet in today's lesson would have stood up and shouted, "Amen!"

AIM

By the end of the lesson, students will be able to express clearly the basic message of Amos to God's people in their pre-exile situation, understand the relationship between Israel's sins and their national decline, understand the importance of holy living as Christians in today's society as a deterrent to our nation's moral decline, and join a Christian church-related organization that is dedicated to the struggle for justice and social uplift.

SCRIPTURE TEXT

> AMOS 4:4 Come to Bethel, and transgress; at Gilgal multiply transgression; and bring your sacrifices every morning, and your tithes after three years:
>
> 5 And offer a sacrifice of thanksgiving with leaven, and proclaim and publish the free offerings: for this liketh you, O ye children of Israel, saith the Lord God.
>
> 5:18 Woe unto you that desire the day of the Lord! to what end is it for you? the day of the Lord is darkness, and not light.
>
> 19 As if a man did flee from a lion, and a bear met him; or went into the house, and leaned his hand on the wall, and a serpent bit him.
>
> 20 Shall not the day of the Lord be darkness, and not light? even very dark, and no brightness in it?
>
> 21 I hate, I despise your feast days, and I will not smell in your solemn assemblies.
>
> 22 Though ye offer me burnt offerings and your meat offerings, I will not accept them: neither will I regard the peace offerings of your fat beasts.
>
> 23 Take thou away from me the noise of thy songs; for I will not hear the melody of thy viols.

24 But let judgment run down as waters, and righteousness as a mighty stream.

BIBLE BACKGROUND

During the prophetic ministry of Amos, Uzziah was king in Judah, and Jeroboam II in Israel. Both kingdoms were prosperous and successful but for different reasons. In the case of Uzziah, the Bible states, "as long as he sought the Lord," he prospered (2 Chronicles 26:5). When he became filled with pride and presumed to take the place of the priest in offering sacrifices, he was struck with leprosy and died a sick, lonely man.

Jeroboam II was noted for continuing idolatrous worship and other sins, yet his reign was prosperous also. He extended "the coast of Israel from the entering of Hamath unto the sea of the plain" (2 Kings 14:25). His prosperity was due to God's promise to Jonah, the prophet, that He would not blot out the name of Israel (v. 27).

Here is a lesson which tells us that we can measure neither God's favor nor our faith by what we possess materially. This is especially important in today's society, where prosperity rather than spiritual maturity has become the standard by which some people determine faith.

It is also difficult for a nation to hear the warnings issued by the Lord in the midst of prosperity and power. Both kingdoms were enjoying great wealth in spite of their backsliding. Amos, Joel, Jonah, and Hosea were prophets during this time. But the people did not want to hear their messages, which called for repentance in the face of impending judgment.

POINTS TO PONDER

1. *What three phrases spoken by Amos can be labeled "sarcastic"? (Amos 4:4-5)*
2. *What did Israel expect to happen on the "great day"? (5:18)*
3. *What did Amos say was going to happen on the "Day of the Lord"? (vv. 18-20)*
4. *What are some of the things that God hates? (vv. 21-23)*
5. *What are the two actions that Amos said God wants? (v. 24)*

LESSON AT-A-GLANCE

1. *The day of rebellion (Amos 4:4, 5)*
2. *The day of retribution (5:18-20)*
3. *The day of rejection (vv. 21-24)*

EXPLORING THE MEANING

1. The day of rebellion (Amos 4:4, 5)

The statements in these two verses are loaded with sarcasm. Both Bethel and Gilgal were considered holy cities. They were places of worship and sacrifice to the true God. Now they had become desecrated places in which idol worship was practiced. They had become centers for the rebellion of God's chosen people. (See *LIGHT ON THE HEAVY* section.)

Still, in the midst of all this rebellion and turning away from God, the people still attended to some form of Jewish worship. God severely chided them for forsaking Him and yet continue in corrupted forms of worship.

We live in ecumenical times. In the name of peace and unity among the world's religions, some Christians have a smile on and then adopt doctrines of non-Christian religions, integrating them into Christianity and contending that they are "keeping the faith." One lesson to be learned from Israel and Judah's mistakes is that Christians cannot practice doctrines not in harmony with the Word of God without suffering the consequences of contamination. Because of their sins, Israel and Judah lost their godly perspective and saw only through their own eyes, which were clouded by the cataracts of self-deception.

2. The day of retribution (5:18-20)

In spite of their numerous acts of rebellion, the people still looked for God to deliver them when they were in trouble. They still looked for the greatest day of deliverance of all: the Day of the Lord. That would be the day when all their enemies would be conquered, and they believed they could once again be the greatest nation on earth.

But Amos warned that the Day of the Lord would not be what they expected. Verses 18 and 20 described it as a day of darkness, not light. A day of woes, not a day of victory and celebration.

To further drive home the negative nature of this day, Amos likened it to a person running from the jaws of a lion and heading right into the paws of a bear. Or, he prophesied, it would be like going into the safety of a house and resting against the walls, only to be attacked by a poisonous snake (v. 19). There will be no escape from judgment on the Day of the Lord.

This might be compared to those who feel God ought to let them into heaven without having received Christ or living a Christian life. Those in the church who believe church membership without heart transformation will guarantee salvation when our Lord returns will be greatly disappointed. The Day of the Lord for the unrighteous will be a day of retribution and judgment, not victory.

A CALL FOR JUSTICE AND RIGHTEOUSNESS

3. The day of rejection (5:21-24)

Through Amos, the Lord also uses strong, negative words to describe His position on His people's continued practice of Jewish ritual: "I hate," He said, "I despise…" (v. 21). Throughout the Book of Amos, there is much repetition of same ideas using different words: "For three transgressions…and for four, I will not turn away the punishment…" (Amos 1:3, 6, 9, 11, 13; 2:1, 4, 6); "I have…yet ye have not returned unto me" (4:6-10); and, "seek…seek" (5:6, 14).

The very things which pleased God in their worship have become despised by Him: their feast days, burnt offerings, meat offerings, peace offerings. He even said that their songs were no longer melodious offerings of worship but a lot of noise that disturbed His ears. The word "noise," in verse 23, is from the Hebrew word *hamon* which means tumult or chaos.

What were these feast days, solemn assemblies, and offerings that the Lord despised? These were very special times God had set aside for worship.

The feasts were of four categories: weekly, monthly, annual, and periodic. The primary *weekly* feast was the SABBATH. This day of rest commemorated both the Lord's rest after the Creation and Israel's deliverance from Egyptian slavery. All work was to cease from sunset Friday to sunset Saturday. According to rabbinic interpretation, a Jew was not to walk more than 1,200 yards, called "a Sabbath Day's journey." The Sabbath was primarily a family celebration, strictly regulated, and some Jews would rather suffer death by being massacred than profane the Sabbath during an attack on that day.

The principal *monthly* feast was the festival of the NEW MOON. Special offerings were demanded by the Law at the beginning of each month (Numbers 28:11-15; Ezra 3:5). David arranged for its celebration by the Levites and it was a prominent feast during the time of the kings (1 Chronicles 23:31).

Five *annual* feasts were observed. 1) The first was the PASSOVER which celebrated God's sparing the Israelites when the death angel passed through Egypt and killed the firstborn children and animals (Exodus 12:11, 21, 27, 43, 48). 2) PENTECOST or the Feast of Weeks (Harvest Festival) is the second annual feast in which certain animals were sacrificed, a freewill offering given, and a celebration observed in which the Levites, foreigners, orphans, widows, were included. 3) The FEAST OF TABERNACLES or BOOTHS FESTIVAL OF SHELTERS came at harvest time and was a seven-day outdoor thanksgiving celebration (Numbers 29:12-40). Booths were made of branches, leaves, willows, and certain fruits to commemorate the children of Israel's years in the wilderness. It was a week when 70 bulls were sacrificed, the Law was read, and families, servants, Levites, orphans, and foreigners came together to eat, rest, and rejoice. 4) THE DAY OF ATONEMENT was a time of rest and fasting (Leviticus 23:26-32). On this day a goat was killed and sent into the wilderness to signify the cleansing and removal of the sins of the priest and people (16:8, 10, 26). 5) The NEW YEAR FESTIVAL or FEAST OF TRUMPETS was a time when Jehovah was symbolically crowned king (Numbers 29:1-6). On those occasions certain "enthronement psalms" were sung (Psalm 47; 93; 96-99).

In addition to the weekly, monthly, and annual feasts, there were also *periodic* festivals. The two that stand out most clearly are the SABBATICAL YEAR and the YEAR OF JUBILEE (Leviticus 25:1-24).

THE SABBATICAL YEAR was celebrated every seven years. During this year, all debts were canceled, no crops were planted, and the land was rested or given a sabbatical. THE YEAR OF

JUBILEE was a time when all slaves were freed, and all property was returned to its original owners. The Jubilee Year began on THE DAY OF ATONEMENT of the 49th year. A trumpet was sounded, and the YEAR OF JUBILEE's theme was freedom.

What were the burnt, meat, and peace offerings of which Amos spoke? The name BURNT offering describes itself. A bull, sheep, goat, ram, lamb, or bird was brought by the presenter. The person was required to place his hand on the animal as a way of identifying with the sacrifice. He then killed it and presented its blood to the priest, who sprinkled it around the altar and burnt the animal on the altar. The smell of the animal went up to the Lord as a pleasing odor and signified the presenter's total surrender to God (Leviticus 1). Burnt offerings were presented twice daily, as well as during the various feasts discussed earlier.

The MEAT offering, also called the cereal or meal offering consisted of a mixture of finely ground flour, olive oil, and frankincense made into cakes and baked. These cakes often accompanied burnt offerings. Half of the cakes brought by the presenters were given to the priests, who burned them with the burnt offerings. The meat gave the burnt offerings a sweet smell. The other half of the cakes were accepted by the priests as gifts from the presenters (Leviticus 2; 6:14-23).

The PEACE offering was a basic component of all communal offerings (Leviticus 3). Normally, peace offerings were not required but were made voluntarily and often accompanied other offerings. The peace sacrifices could be animals or unleavened cakes. Perhaps the outstanding feature of this is that it ended with a communal meal which could include the presenter, his family, and the Levites in his community. (See J. P. Lewis, "Feasts," *Pictorial Encyclopedia of the Bible*, Volume II, 1976, pp. 521-525.)

Having briefly reviewed the feasts and offerings mentioned by Amos, what was his problem? After all, these rituals were instituted by God.

There seem to have been two basic problems. The first was that after the Jews offered their sacrifices to Jehovah in the temple, they would then go and offer sacrifices to Baal also. To Amos, a sacrifice was not just a ritual, it was a commitment—a declaration of exclusive loyalty to the God who had been so loyal to His people. To Amos, this double offering of sacrifices was spiritual adultery. It was synonymous to a married person sleeping with his or her spouse one night, and then sleeping with his or her neighbor's spouse the next night. This lack of loyalty was Amos' first problem with his people.

His second problem was that after they finished these feasts and offerings, accompanied by beautiful vocal and instrumental music, they went out and made life a living hell for their less fortunate brothers and sisters. After all the beautiful worship, they went out and "trample(d) on the poor" and "oppress(ed) the righteous" (Amos 5:11-12, NIV).

Amos had the old-fashioned belief that worship was supposed to make a difference in a person's life. He believed that worship should make the worshiper better—spiritually, morally, and socially.

And according to Jesus, he was right. Jesus said, "And why call ye me, Lord, Lord, and do not the things which I say?" (Luke 6:46, KJV). He taught that the Judgment Day test is not going to be whether we went faithfully to Sunday morning worship services, but how we treated hungry, naked, imprisoned, and sick people (Matthew 25:31 ff.).

Jesus indicated that if the choice is between going faithfully to church and helping a poor, robbed, beaten stranger on some

A CALL FOR JUSTICE AND RIGHTEOUSNESS

Jericho road in Palestine, or State Street in Chicago, or Crenshaw Boulevard in West Los Angeles, we should stop and help the stranger (Luke 10:25-37). That's why the Lord said through a very distressed Amos:

> "I hate, I despise your religious festivals;
>
> your assemblies are a stench to me.
>
> Away with the noise of your songs!
>
> I will not listen to the music of your harps." (Amos 5:21, 23, NIV)
>
> Well, Lord, what do You want?

He answered: "I want justice and righteousness. I want you to treat people fair and I want you to do it because your heart is right with me" (5:24, paraphrased).

Is there a message here for 20th century African Americans? We have demanded that others treat us justly. How are we treating each other?

DISCERNING MY DUTY

1. *Understanding the functions of the cities of Bethel and Gilgal, why would Amos invite the Israelites to these cities, to "come and transgress"?*

2. *Do you think that Reverend Amos (see the DEFINING THE ISSUE section) was right in not allowing his choir to continue singing? What two or three other specific steps can he take to help the choir become more Christ-like in their personal lives?*

3. *Do you believe any church leader should be able to exercise authority in church if he or she is "living in sin"?*
4. *What are two or three specific ways that your church can promote justice in the community surrounding the church?*

DECIDING MY RESPONSE

To think about—1. Throughout history, the governing and religious systems of nations have been intimately related. In the case of Judaism and Christianity, this relationship sometimes created higher moral standards. How has the recent call in America for removal of various religious practices affected the morality of our nation?

2. In a country that has many cultures and many religions, is it proper to insist on public religious practices that are exclusively Christian?

3. If you had to file a status report with the Lord on the state of your church, so that God could determine the "blessing budget" for the coming year, what would you say in your report? For what strengths would you commend your church? What weaknesses would you point out for correction?

To do—Are you a member of either the NAACP, PUSH, or UNCF? While these are not strictly religious organizations, they do have committees on which church folk serve. Seriously consider joining one of these social organizations. Through them you can be used by God.

WHAT I WILL DO

_____
_____
_____

LIGHT ON THE HEAVY

BETHEL ("House of God"). Bethel was located in Palestine, about 10 miles north of Jerusalem. Originally known as Luz (Genesis 28:19), it was a city where, in troubled times, people went to ask the counsel of God (Judges 20:18, 31; 21:2). The ark of the covenant once rested there (Judges 20:26-28). Later, idolatrous worship was practiced in Bethel (1 Kings 12:28-33; 13:1). Hosea (Hosea 10:5) called it "Beth Aven" in contempt for the trespasses of God's people. King Josiah managed to stop idolatry there, temporarily (2 Kings 23:15-18), and the city was still in existence after the Babylonian captivity.

GILGAL ("Rolling"). Gilgal was located on the plains of Jericho and is the place where the Israelites first encamped after crossing the Jordan River (Joshua 4:19, 20). It was the place where the first Passover was celebrated after the Exodus. Gilgal was one of the three towns in which Samuel did his judging and offered sacrifices (1 Samuel 7:16). It later became a place of idolatry (Hosea 4:15).

God Promises to Bless
Based on Ezekiel 34:11-31

DEFINING THE ISSUE

Can you recall a time in your life when you found yourself dependent on someone else for your care, guidance, and protection? Most of us would say, "Of course, I can remember the times when I was a child." But how about the times when you were an adult, and life was too much for you to handle? All of us have gone through those periods when we felt helpless and needed someone to lean on.

At other times we have found ourselves responsible for caring, guiding, and protecting others. How did you feel about it? Did caring for others make you glad or mad? Sometimes we don't want the responsibility of helping others, although we want the acknowledgment from people who see our "good works."

No doubt many of us have also experienced the hurt and disappointment when those in leadership positions have not only failed to perform their duties, but also misused their power and position for their own personal gain, even at the expense of those they are supposedly helping. The old South African government is a prime example of this. There were people in key political and religious positions in that country who made decisions which robbed Black people of their God-given rights and privileges.

This week's lesson will look at God's Word spoken through the Prophet Ezekiel regarding the kings and the Israelites who had neglected their responsibilities to each other. God chose the motif of a shepherd and sheep to describe the type of relationship He wants to have with His people. We will also learn how people neglect their responsibilities to each other, and how we can also avoid disappointment when our leaders fall short of their responsibilities or miss the mark. It is a word of judgment for those who are oppressors and a word of hope for those being oppressed.

AIM

By the end of the lesson, students will recognize that God is the source of their blessings in every aspect of life, and they will sense the need to share with others some of the blessings God has bestowed on them.

SCRIPTURE TEXT

> EZEKIEL 34:17 And as for you, O my flock, thus saith the Lord God; Behold, I judge between cattle and cattle, between the rams and the he goats.
>
> 20 Therefore thus saith the Lord God unto them; Behold, I, even I, will judge between the fat cattle and between the lean cattle.
>
> 21 Because ye have thrust with side and with shoulder, and pushed all the diseased with your horns, till ye have scattered them abroad;
>
> 22 Therefore will I save my flock, and they shall no more be a prey; and I will judge between cattle and cattle.

23 And I will set up one shepherd over them, and he shall feed them, even my servant David; he shall feed them, and he shall be their shepherd.

24 And I the Lord will be their God, and my servant David a prince among them; I the Lord have spoken it.

25 And I will make with them a covenant of peace, and will cause the evil beasts to cease out of the land: and they shall dwell safely in the wilderness, and sleep in the woods.

26 And I will make them and the places round about my hill a blessing; and I will cause the shower to come down in his season; there shall be showers of blessing.

27 And the tree of the field shall yield her fruit, and the earth shall yield her increase, and they shall be safe in their land, and shall know that I am the Lord, when I have broken the bands of their yoke, and delivered them out of the hand of those that served themselves of them.

28 And they shall no more be a prey to the heathen, neither shall the beast of the land devour them; but they shall dwell safely, and none shall make them afraid.

29 And I will raise up for them a plant of renown, and they shall be no more consumed with hunger in the land, neither bear the shame of the heathen any more.

30 Thus shall they know that I the Lord their God am with them, and that they, even the house of Israel, are my people, saith the Lord God.

31 And ye my flock, the flock of my pasture, are men, and I am your God, saith the Lord God.

BIBLE BACKGROUND

The people of Israel tried to blame their predicament on the sins of their fathers from a generation past. But God made it clear that each person would be judged for his or her own sins and not the sins of someone else. What God wanted more than anything was for the people to repent of their ways and live according to His Word (see Ezekiel 18:30-31).

This text zeroes in on a specific sin the people were committing, and God holds them accountable for it on an individual basis. The Israelites from the Southern Kingdom were at an all-time low politically. They had witnessed the destruction of their homeland and of God's temple by the Babylonians. They were now living in captivity in a foreign land with little hope of being free again. During this time, Ezekiel (whose name means "God strengthens") had been chosen by God to relay a word of judgment and hope to the people.

The first segment of the scriptural passage pronounces God's judgment on those leaders or kings who disregarded the people's needs for their own personal pleasure (see Ezekiel 34:1-10). Some people believe that the "kings" mentioned are the disobedient kings of Israel whose actions resulted in the punishment of captivity. Others think that the "shepherds" are the Israelites' foreign captors being judged.

The second section of the warning condemns those who have taken on the attitude of their leaders, but it also speaks of blessings for those who have fallen victim to the leaders' arrogant attitude (see 34:11-17). This is where our lesson begins.

POINTS TO PONDER

1. *Who was God going to judge and for what reason? (Ezekiel 34:17, 20-22)*
2. *How had the shepherds neglected the flock? (v. 21)*
3. *Who was the shepherd that God was going to send to feed the people? (vv. 23-24)*
4. *As a result of God's provision, what was going to happen to the sheep? (vv. 25-29)*
5. *Why was God going to do all of this for His people? (vv. 30-31)*

LESSON AT-A-GLANCE

1. *Hope for the flock (Ezekiel 34:17, 20-24)*
   A. *Judgment of the flock (vv. 17, 20-22)*
   B. *A shepherd assigned (vv. 23-24)*
2. *Needs of the flock met (vv. 25-29)*
3. *The people will know their God (vv. 30-31)*

EXPLORING THE MEANING

1. Hope for the flock (Ezekiel 34:17, 20-24)

A. *Judgment of the flock (vv. 17, 20-22)*

During Ezekiel's time, kings were often referred to as shepherds in Judah (see Jeremiah 10:21; 23:1-4; Ezekiel 34:1-10), and the children of Israel were like sheep. The "shepherds" had not taken care of the flock, and God had already passed a "woe" on them (34:2). In this passage God addresses the flock who abused one another. There would also be judgment between cattle and cattle, and between rams and he goats (v. 17).

The fat cattle (v. 20) refers to the rich and powerful who applied tactics on the weak and poor ("the lean cattle") meant to do them harm. Instead of using their wealth and authority to meet the needs of the "diseased" (v. 21), they pushed them aside and used their influence and power to feed only themselves. So, what does God say He will do? He will offer divine protection to His flock, so they will no longer be a prey to the "fat cattle." He will also judge between the "cattle" to see what has been done to help the poor.

How do we treat those in our society who are economically disadvantaged or mentally or physically handicapped? Do we avoid them, hoping they'll go away? Do we take advantage of them just because we can? African American people are very familiar with such treatment, and yet we can be insensitive to others who are less fortunate than us. We need to be careful that we don't misuse anyone.

When God said He will judge, what did He mean? There are several meanings to the Hebrew word "to judge" (*shaphat*). One refers to the action of a third party who sits over two parties in conflict with one another. Another meaning denotes delivery from injustice or oppression. Yet another is the process by which law and order are maintained within a group (*An Expositor's Dictionary of Bible Words*, Thomas Nelson Publishers, 1984, pp. 204-205). God's judgment seems to encompass all three meanings. His Word also indicates that we must do what we can to draw the disadvantaged closer to us, so that we might help them. In order for us to do so, however, we must reject society's general philosophy, which is to get all we can for ourselves. Instead, let's reach out and be more concerned about a brother or sister in need.

B. A Shepherd assigned (vv. 23-24)

Chapter 34 of Ezekiel is known as the "restoration" chapter. Israel had been a united kingdom under King David's rule. But now Ezekiel reminds the enslaved nation of how things were before they were separated as a nation and taken away from the land. Ezekiel reminds the people that one day God would raise up a leader who would be worthy and able to save the people from their predicament and feed them and bring them back to Him.

This "shepherd" (v. 23) was of the Davidic dynasty and was viewed as the "Messianic King," Jesus Christ, the Good Shepherd (see John 10:11). While other shepherds failed to feed and satisfy the people, this Shepherd would provide and care for them forever.

Sometimes we expect too much from our leaders and depend on them for everything. We look to them to provide what only God can. We must remember what the Bible says: "But my God shall supply all your need according to his riches in glory by Christ Jesus" (Philippians 4:19). We can't look to the preachers or the missionaries to provide for us. If Christ is our Shepherd, He is the One to whom we should turn. Let's see what we can expect from our Shepherd as we look to Him.

2. Needs of the flock met (vv. 25-29)

Just as a shepherd protects his sheep and leads them to a place where they can graze without fear, so will God provide for His people. Ezekiel tells them that God will make a "covenant of peace" (v. 25) with them, which implies that they will have an active role in the agreement. So it is with us. When we accept Jesus Christ as our Shepherd, we can look forward to a promise of peace in three dimensions. When we receive all that God is providing for us we will have: (1) peace physically, free from bodily harm; (2) peace mentally, peace of mind; and (3) peace spiritually, free from the bondage of sin. Temptation will have no power over us.

The spiritual peace we are to experience will eventually take place in Zion, the city of David, or Jerusalem, which is often referred to as "the hill of the Lord" and which signifies that God's presence and holiness will be there.

God has also promised that He will shower down His blessings on His people (v. 26). The primary meaning of the Hebrew verb "to bless" is to bend the knees. But there are three other uses of the word which have developed over time. The first use of the term involves worship, adoration, or praise of Him. The second use indicates favor and goodness that God bestows on men and women. Once we receive the blessings of God, then we can call forth the same for each other, and this is the word's third usage (*The Interpreter's Dictionary of the Bible*, Abingdon Press, 1984, p. 445).

God also promises to provide food and nourishment for the people and safety in the land once again (v. 27). When they experience this, they will know that it was He who broke the yokes of bondage they were under and delivered them from their oppressors.

Some people tend to be impatient and intolerant with those who have special needs. But just as God promises to bestow physical and spiritual goodness on us, we should respond by sharing what we have received from Him with others.

A story is told of a church member who died and was met by an angel who, prior to taking him to heaven, allowed him to see hell. The person saw a large room with many tables. On each table sat a large pot of stew. Standing along the walls were hundreds of weak, thin, and sorrowful people holding spoons that were too long for them. "This is terrible, the spoons are too long, and the people can't reach the stew or eat it," said the man. "Well, that's how hell is," was the angel's reply. The angel took the man to heaven where there was another large room with many tables. On each table sat a large pot of stew. There were people standing along the walls holding spoons, but they were laughing and everyone looked healthy and full of joy. The man asked the angel, "What's going on here? Why are these people so healthy and happy even though they are standing along the wall as the others I first saw?" The angel told the man, "Here in heaven the people feed each other so they are always full of joy." As God provides for us, we ought to provide for one another.

The people will be freed from oppression, and no nation will ever be able to enslave them again once God's Shepherd has come. They will dwell in safety, and no one will be able to do them harm anymore. So it is with us. God has sent His Son Jesus into the world to break the yokes of sin and deliver us from spiritual oppression. Because we are free, we can show unbelievers the way to freedom.

3. The people will know their God (vv. 30-31)
Once the people have been delivered from the yokes of bondage and been restored to their land, they will know who God is. For He is the Master Shepherd, and they are the sheep of His pasture (v. 31).

"Thus shall they know…" (v. 30). The result of recognizing God as the source of all of our needs is spiritual insight. When we think of all the people who are not spiritually aware of God, we can be grateful for the relationship we have with Him. It is a blessing to know we are part of God's "flock." The more spiritual insight we gain about who God is and what He can do for us, the more we will love Him and desire to live out His will every day. The key is to hold on to God's promises and not let go. He has promised to bless His people.

DISCERNING MY DUTY

1. *How is God's judgment different from ours?*
2. *How does God "feed and shepherd" us? Be specific.*
3. *What are the showers of blessings God provides for us?*
4. *Who are our oppressors? What can we do to break the yokes of bondage that are around our people? Give examples.*
5. *What are some specific ways we can bless people we come in contact with? Give examples.*

DECIDING MY RESPONSE

To think about—How can we challenge leaders to be more compassionate to those they lead? Give some specific suggestions that can be shared with the leaders of your church.

To do—This week, as you reflect on this lesson, give some thought as to how you can be a blessing to another person. Perhaps you might share a word of comfort or help someone in need. Whatever you do, make it tangible.

WHAT I WILL DO

_____
_____
_____
_____

LIGHT ON THE HEAVY

DAVID. His name means "beloved." The great-grandson of Ruth and Boaz. He was the youngest of eight brothers and was brought up as a shepherd, during which he learned about courage. His courage later became evident in battle (see 1 Samuel 17:34-35). David also learned about tenderness and care for his flock, which he later sung about as attributes of his God.

David reigned as King of Israel for 40 years. He led the Israelites in battle against their enemies and brought back the ark of the covenant (see 2 Samuel 6:2). At the height of David's prosperity and religious fervor, he committed the sin referred to as "the matter of Uriah the Hittite" (see 2 Samuel 11), which is an example of how sin can spoil God's purpose for His children. It is safe to say that David was viewed as the normative king, but the prophecy of Nathan (see 2 Samuel 7:12-16) does not definitely require one king as its fulfillment. Nathan predicted a stable house, kingdom, and throne for David.

As failure set in from Solomon's last years on, the days of David glowed brighter in Israel's memory, and hope became envisioned as the "David" of the future, Jesus Christ. (*The New Bible Dictionary*, Tyndale Publishing House, 1984, pp. 265, 268, 765-766)

God Gives New Life
Based on Ezekiel 37:1-14

DEFINING THE ISSUE

Ken and his wife Sheila were at a soul food restaurant in the Bedford-Stuyvesant section of Brooklyn a few weeks ago after church. They were enjoying a good meal of greens, corn on the cob, sweet potatoes, and fried chicken, when suddenly Ken grabbed his throat. He had swallowed a chicken bone and it was lodged in his esophagus.

Quick as lightning Sheila jumped to her feet and raced behind him. She immediately grabbed his mid-section with both arms and balled up her fist and pressed it against his stomach. After a few sudden jerks from Sheila, the bone was forced out of Ken's mouth. After that she began administering CPR (cardiac pulmonary resuscitation) until Ken was able to catch his breath.

There is a growing concern in our society that many people should learn CPR so they will be prepared for emergency situations.

When the heart or lungs of someone have stopped working, there are specific steps a person can take to get those organs to operate again. First, it is advised to remove anything that can block the flow of air from the victim's mouth. Next, you tilt the head back, pinch the nostrils shut, place your mouth over the victim's, and blow until his/her chest rises. Then, listen for air being exhaled from the person. Finally, apply external cardiac compression to force blood from the heart to flow through the pulmonary arteries to other parts of the body. It is advised that these steps be performed by two people (*The Johnson and Johnson First Aid Book*, Warner Books, 1985).

Today's lesson is about a nation of people who had lost all hope and were, for all practical purposes, dead. In a vision, God told Ezekiel that He would perform CPR (Calvary Plus Resurrection) on a dead nation of people and bring them back to life.

We all experience a loss of hope in our lives at one time or another. But we can learn definite steps from this lesson that can help us revive our "dead" souls as we look to God in our times of need.

AIM

By the end of the lesson, students will learn that God gives new vitality to every area of their lives, regardless of what they may be going through.

SCRIPTURE TEXT

> EZEKIEL 37:3 And he said unto me, Son of man, can these bones live? And I answered, O Lord God, thou knowest.
>
> 4 Again he said unto me, Prophesy upon these bones, and say unto them, O ye dry bones, hear the word of the Lord.
>
> 5 Thus saith the Lord God unto these bones; Behold, I will cause breath to enter into you, and ye shall live:

6 And I will lay sinews upon you, and will bring up flesh upon you, and cover you with skin, and put breath in you, and ye shall live; and ye shall know that I am the Lord.

7 So I prophesied as I was commanded: and as I prophesied, there was a noise, and behold a shaking, and the bones came together, bone to his bone.

8 And when I beheld, lo, the sinews and the flesh came up upon them, and the skin covered them above: but there was no breath in them.

9 Then said he unto me, Prophesy unto the wind, prophesy, son of man, and say to the wind, Thus saith the Lord God; Come from the four winds, O breath, and breathe upon these slain, that they may live.

10 So I prophesied as he commanded me, and the breath came into them, and they lived, and stood up upon their feet, an exceeding great army.

11 Then he said unto me, Son of man, these bones are the whole house of Israel: behold, they say, Our bones are dried, and our hope is lost: we are cut off for our parts.

12 Therefore prophesy and say unto them, Thus saith the Lord God; Behold, O my people, I will open your graves, and cause you to come up out of your graves, and bring you into the land of Israel.

13 And ye shall know that I am the Lord, when I have opened your graves, O my people, and brought you up out of your graves,

14 And shall put my spirit in you, and ye shall live, and I shall place you in your own land: then shall ye know that I the Lord have spoken it, and performed it, saith the Lord.

BIBLE BACKGROUND

God had promised to bless His people by establishing a relationship with them like that of a shepherd with his flock. As a result of God's blessing, they would in turn bless one another.

God was ready to rebuild Israel and to establish a new covenant with His people. He was ready to put a new spirit in them (36:23-27) and to cleanse them from all unrighteousness and iniquities (see 36:33-34). God wanted the other nations around them to know of His sovereignty, and He wanted Israel to know the same thing.

In this study, God promises to put His spirit into the flock. The lesson begins with Ezekiel's vision where he was set down in a valley of bones (see 37:1-2).

Valleys were often the scene for battles, and God "carries" Ezekiel into a valley of the bones of a defeated army, symbolic of the Hebrew nation. We can conclude from these scattered dry bones that they had been there a very long time, since the flesh had decayed. The divided, scattered nation of Israel was in captivity to the Babylonians for about 70 years, and they had little hope of going back to their homeland. They were surrounded by a people who bowed to pagan gods and participated in temple prostitution. Their spirituality had expired. How, in this state, were they going to look to the Shepherd and be shepherds to each other?

When we look at leaders like Martin Luther King, Jr. and what they tried to do for all people, and then look at where we are now and where we should be as a nation of people, are we like a valley of dry bones, of a defeated army in a valley of despair? We need to remember that as long as God is on our side, there is hope.

POINTS TO PONDER

1. *Where was Ezekiel when he saw the vision of the "dry bones"? (Ezekiel 34:1)*
2. *Why did God ask Ezekiel, "can these bones live again"? (v. 3)*
3. *Why did Ezekiel have to speak to the bones? (vv. 4, 7)*
4. *What did God promise He would do for the bones? (vv. 5, 6, 12-14)*
5. *Who did the bones represent? (v. 11)*

LESSON AT-A-GLANCE

1. *The vision of dry bones (Ezekiel 37:3-10)*
   A. *God uses Ezekiel (vv. 3-6)*
   B. *Ezekiel obeys God (vv. 7-10)*
2. *The vision explained (vv. 11-14)*
   A. *Israel returns home (vv. 11-13)*
   B. *Israel is revived (v. 14)*

EXPLORING THE MEANING

1. **The vision of dry bones (Ezekiel 37:3-10)**

    A. *God uses Ezekiel (vv. 3-6)*

    As Ezekiel viewed the valley of dry bones (v. 1), God asked him a question: "Son of man, can these bones live?" (v. 3a) God wanted to know what Ezekiel thought and whether he was really prepared for the task. After looking at the bones and determining they were very dry, Ezekiel could conclude only one thing. If these bones were going to live again, only one Person had knowledge to know and the power to make it happen. Though it seemed a hopeless situation to Ezekiel, his answer rung loud and clear, "Lord, you alone know the answer to that" (v. 3b, LB).

When we are faced with a seemingly hopeless situation, do we doubt God's ability to perform great miracles? God does not want us to doubt ourselves or Him. Even though we may face seemingly impossible situations, the Bible tells us, "with God all things are possible" (Matthew 19:26, NIV).

Though Ezekiel replied, "O Lord God, you know," it would appear that he was not in despair because he had hope in God. Therefore, God did not doubt Ezekiel's ability to prophesy. As a matter of fact, it would be the prophecy of Ezekiel that would bring the "bones" back to life. Ezekiel was commanded to tell the bones to hear the word of the Lord, who would bring the nation of Israel back to life.

God "caused breath" to enter into the bones so they would live (v. 6). The Hebrew word used here for breath is *ruach*, which also means spirit and wind. This suggests that God's promise to the nation exceeded mere physical revival (such as happened in Genesis 2:7 when God "breathed" into Adam and he became a living soul). What God refers to is a spiritual revival which will cause the nation to know and understand His ways and then "live" again.

Without the Spirit of God operating in our lives, there is no way we can acknowledge Him (see 1 Corinthians 12:3) or understand the things of the Lord (see 1 Corinthians 2:12). As a matter of fact, without the Spirit of God operating in us, we can't even say we are His (see Romans 8:9). It is the Spirit that gives us abundant life so that we might discern the things of the Lord and be all He wants us to be.

God was going to do a supernatural work so the "bones" could come together again. They were scattered across the valley, and it would be the Word of the Lord that would bring them together again.

B. *Ezekiel obeys God (vv. 7-10)*

Obedience and faith in God can enable us to perform great miracles for Him. If we are obedient in using the spiritual gifts God gave us for His glory, we can be an instrument by which God gives others new life.

Ezekiel did as he was told and prophesied to the bones. As he spoke, a miracle took place. The bones began to come together, so they were no longer scattered everywhere. When we think of bones, we think of the hard substance which forms the framework of the human body. It is interesting to note that the bone is the most active tissue in the body; it cleanses the blood of harmful substances.

The coming together of the bones (v. 7) signifies the coming together of the once divided and scattered Hebrew nation. The power of God's Word can bring a nation of people together again to actively participate in His will, purifying the world in the process. Ezekiel also saw muscles, flesh, and skin come upon the bones.

Muscles move the bones by pulling on the tendons. The skin regulates body heat by way of the sweat glands. Therefore, it seems that God is giving the people all they need to perform physically. But they won't be able to do so unless the

Spirit of God is within the body. Ezekiel was commanded to prophesy to the wind in its fullest state, since it was to come from the four corners of the earth. Once the "wind" entered them, they came alive and became "an exceeding great army" (v. 10). Were the bones ready to go? No, they still didn't have "life," or the Spirit within.

No one can do anything, regardless of what gifts he or she may possess, without the Spirit of God. This "intake" of breath makes the difference as to whether we will be successful in doing whatever the Lord desires of us.

2. The vision explained (vv. 11-14)

A. Israel returns home (vv. 11-13)

Now we learn what the vision was all about. After the bones rise from the dead God tells Ezekiel that they represent the whole household of Israel. They had lost hope, they were cut off from their land, and, as a result, they were "dead." But God responds by promising to remove the people from the captivity of the heathen land, quench their dry spirits with the living waters of His Spirit, and put them in their own land.

The grave was no longer a place for a resurrected people who were filled with the Spirit of God. Therefore, the Israelites had to be removed from the land of Babylon and taken to a land of their own, where they would have the freedom to worship the true and living God. When this happens there will be no doubt in the people's mind who has done it. Therefore, only He deserves and receives the glory for His marvelous work in their lives.

It is important that we praise the Lord with our whole hearts when He touches our spirits and we receive a fresh anointing from Him. Only God is able to lift us from the "graves" of depression and sadness, and place our feet on the Solid Rock, Jesus Christ.

B. *Israel is revived (v. 14)*

Once God placed the Israelites in their land, He promised to fill them with His Spirit. The people will be aware that He is in control. His Spirit will dwell in the people, individually and collectively, giving them new life.

Let's review what steps were taken for the people to reach this point: First, there was an obedient and faithful prophet who used his gift to edify the people. Next, there was a nation of people who, because of their disobedience, were captured and became spiritually dead. God used Ezekiel to perform "CPR" to revive them. They were removed from the situation which prevented the flow of God's Spirit from entering them. Then, God enabled them to look up to Him and receive His Spirit so they could have new life.

Jesus Christ transcended time when He applied external cardiac compression by dying on the cross. CPR applied by Christ and the Holy Spirit gives us everlasting life that we may never have to die again.

So, whatever "grave" we're buried in today, God can give us CPR—Christ's Power through Resurrection!

DISCERNING MY DUTY

1. *What "graves" are people buried in today? Explain.*
2. *What is the significance of God's Spirit in people individually and collectively?*

3. How would you describe the collective spirituality of the African American community and what contributes to it? How does your individual spirituality fit in? Be specific.
4. What can be done to revitalize the "dry bones" in our community so people can take an active part in changing the conditions around them? Be specific.

DECIDING MY RESPONSE

This week, examine your personal weaknesses and strengths. Think of ways you can apply the Word of God to your own situation so that you may grow. Share your findings with someone else who may be going through trials and tribulations.

WHAT I WILL DO

_____
_____
_____

LIGHT ON THE HEAVY

PROPHECY. Prophecy is related to the Hebrew word *nabu* which in its passive form means "to be called." It is used most frequently to describe the function of the true prophet as he speaks God's message to the people, under the influence of the Divine Spirit. "To prophesy" is much more than predicting future events. It contains God's Word to the people calling them to a covenant of faithfulness. The prophet's message is conditional and depends on the response of the people. Thus, by their response to the word, the people greatly determine what the future holds. (*An Expository Dictionary of Biblical Words*, Thomas Nelson Publishers, 1984, pp. 310-311)

SON OF MAN. "Son of Man" is a term for man; human being; an apocalyptic figure; and, in the New Testament, a title for Jesus Christ. The form is used frequently in Ezekiel as God's address to the prophet, and here it must mean, "O man." (*The Interpreter's Dictionary of the Bible*, Abingdon Press, 1984, p. 413)

ABOUT THE AUTHOR

Dr. Melvin E. Banks is the founder of Urban Ministries, Inc., the largest African-American Christian media and content provider, serving over 50,000 churches with curriculum, books, magazines, Bible studies, videos, teaching resources, and more.

Alabama native Dr. Banks began his spiritual journey at the age of 12, sharing Bible stories with younger children and traveling with his mentor to Birmingham's remote parts to give his testimony to adults. Inspired by Hosea 4:6, where God says, "My people are destroyed from lack of knowledge," he established UMI in 1970 to publish positive images of African-Americans in the biblical experience. During its first 12 years, UMI operated from the basement of the Banks' home, and Dr. Banks marketed his first Sunday School curriculum, *InTeen*, to churches out of his car's trunk.

Dr. Banks received an honorary doctorate from his alma mater, Wheaton College, where he served as a trustee for many years. Moody Bible Institute honored him as an Alumnus of the year, and Dr. Banks was recognized for his achievements by the History Makers Foundation.

Today UMI's innovative work has led to many publishers becoming more ethnically and racially diverse in their efforts. Materials include Sunday School curriculum, Vacation Bible School resources, books, videos, music, and website UrbanFaith.com – all of which speak to people of color in the context of their culture. For more information, please visit UrbanMinistries.com.

www.ingramcontent.com/pod-product-compliance
Lightning Source LLC
Chambersburg PA
CBHW031118080526
44587CB00011B/1022